Groomed for Greatness

"A Primer for Personal Purpose"

Solutions for Life Transformation

Dr. Kris F. Erskine

GROOMED FOR GREATNESS
"A Primer for Personal Purpose"

Solutions for Life Transformation

Dr. Kris F. Erskine

All rights reserved. No part of this book shall be reproduced or transmitted in any form or by any means, electronic, mechanical, magnetic, photographic including photocopying, recording or by any information storage and retrieval system, without prior written permission of the publisher. No patent liability is assumed with respect to the use of the information contained herein. Although every precaution has been taken in the preparation of this book, the publisher and author assume no responsibility for errors or omissions. Neither is any liability assumed for damages resulting from the use of the information contained herein.

Copyright © 2015 by Dr. Kris F. Erskine

ISBN 978-1-4958-0738-1

This is a work of fiction. Names, characters, places, and incidents either are the product of the author's imagination or are used fictitiously. Any resemblance to actual events or locales or persons, living or dead, is entirely coincidental.

Published August 2015

INFINITY PUBLISHING
1094 New DeHaven Street, Suite 100
West Conshohocken, PA 19428-2713
Toll-free (877) BUY BOOK
Local Phone (610) 941-9999
Fax (610) 941-9959
Info@buybooksontheweb.com
www.buybooksontheweb.com

DEDICATION

To every person that aspires for greatness, and this primer will assist in attaining goals, standards, and benchmarks for success.

To my spiritual father, mentor, and pastor, Dr. T.L. Lewis, whose visionary leadership, untiring activism, compassion as a husband, devotion as a son, and outstanding Pastoral leadership challenges me daily to strive for greatness.

To my friend and brother Dr. Chance Lewis who challenged me to vacillate into the vein of writing, even before I ever knew I had been gifted to do so. I respect you more than you know. Much love to Mechael, Myra, and Sydney.

To my countless mentees, globally, who privilege me constantly to speak into their lives consistently, I am eternally grateful for your trust in me.

To Bethel-Nation, St. Andrews North Birmingham, Shiloh Baptist Bryan/College Station, TX, and Bethany Baptist Church Harlem, all of whom granted me the opportunity to establish friendships that have stood the test of times. I am made better because of so many.

To Mr. Leotha & Ruby Gaines and the Gaines Family who accepted me over 20 years ago into one of the most loving/supportive families.

To the entire Erskine family who have individually and collectively played major roles in my life. I would not be who I am today without you.

Acknowledgments

Kris F. Erskine, Th.D

This work is the result of a lifetime of learning from multifarious classrooms across the span of my human existence. Many mentors, mentees, teachers, supporters, advisors, pastors, counselors, friends, and family, have invested their time, talent, and treasures, in my life. For this, I am eternally grateful.

No triumph in life is devoid of the assistance of others. We are all the recipients of many known and unknown individuals who have contributed to our lives. Each of us are the sum total of what we have learned from others, and we owe any measure of success to the array of input, advice, and guidance to so many. Here are just a few who assisted in making this work a reality:

To my wife, Loretta, for your love, loyalty, and lifetime commitment to being the "biggest fan" I have. Your support always undergirded with sacrifice, is a treasure that I will forever appreciate.

To Kristian and Alayna, my greatest accomplishment to date. To serve as your father will always be atop the list of accolades and awards I have and will receive throughout my life.

To My mother, Minister Donno Erskine, thank you for speaking life into me from the beginning of my existence. Your prayers have penetrated through pain and produced a purpose that will make your name great.

To My brother Sidell Erskine, many thanks for being the prototype that developed the dedication for this primer. Best Brother Ever!

Contents

Preface- "From Assessment to Achievement" 1

Introduction- You are Great, Now Believe It and Prove It Daily! 5

Chapter 1- Assessments 9
"It's hard to be a diamond in a rhinestone world." — Dolly Parton

Chapter 2- Attitude 17
"When you're good at something, you'll tell everyone. When you're great at something, they'll tell you." — Walter Payton

Chapter 3- Accountability 25
"When your persona gets bigger than your person, then who you have become will kill who you are" — Bishop T.D. Jakes

Chapter 4- Agendas 31
"When you are destined for greatness, it shows in everything you do. It becomes you. Greatness becomes you." — Lori Myers, 3 Off the Tee: Targeting Success

Chapter 5- Adversity 41
"Great spirits have always encountered violent opposition from mediocre minds." — Albert Einstein

Chapter 6- Affirmation 51
"Not everybody can be famous but everybody can be great, because greatness is determined by service." — Martin Luther King

Chapter 7- Achievement 61
"You were put on this earth to achieve your greatest self, to live out your purpose, and to do it fearlessly." — Steve Maraboli, Life, the Truth, and Being Free

Chapter 8- Accomplishment 71
"To be yourself in a world that is constantly trying to make you something else is the greatest accomplishment." — Ralph Waldo Emerson

Taking Action- "Who Is Next" 87

A Word from the Author..93

About the Author..95

Preface
"From Assessment to Achievement"

"Be not afraid of greatness. Some are born great, some achieve greatness, and others have greatness thrust upon them." — William Shakespeare, 12th Night

In researching and designing the cover for "Groomed for Greatness" I found these most exhilarating photos of a lion's first interaction with his young cubs. Lisa Granshaw reported for the TODAY Show on Aug. 22, 2012 at 12:14 PM this article associated with the photographs selected for this project. Here is an excerpt:

This priceless moment captured by wildlife photographer Suzi Eszterhas on Kenya's Masai Mara National Reserve had us all "awwing" in the office. After following a pride of lions for three months, Eszterhas snapped these shots of a male lion meeting his son for the first time.

According to Eszterhas, the curious 7-week-old cub and his siblings had never met their dad before, having been kept in a den under the watchful eye of their mom since birth. Only when the cubs became too big and rowdy for Mom to handle alone does she cautiously let them out and introduce them to the rest of the pride, including their father.

"What's cool about this is, because they've been tucked away in the den, taking them out is this dramatic moment," Eszterhas told TODAY.com.

Capturing the tender father-and-son interaction was very rewarding for the wildlife photographer, who spent a lot of time watching the lions over the course of months.

"This was one of the most memorable moments of my career," she said. "[I'm] out in these long hours and then this amazing moment happens when the cub coyly walks up to his big father."

The lioness still kept a watchful eye on the pride members that interacted with her kids — even when it comes to dad, Eszterhas said.

The Lion is known as "King of the Jungle" and well respected as so. The lion is a magnificent animal that appears as a symbol of power, courage and nobility on family crests, coats of arms and national flags in many civilizations. Lions are quite possibly one of the most fascinating creatures in the world. With their stereotypical ferocious outer appearance yet a soft, community driven spirit, it is no wonder that lions are used as metaphors to represent sporting teams, community centers and countries alike.

While the pictorial lesson from the cover references seem simplistic, they are very philosophical. The cub is at play, although the lion is parenting. The cute cub is enjoying the experience of a lifetime, whereas the lion is ever watchful of dangerous prey that desire to snatch the life from its precious, yet innocent, son. Those that desire to strip the life from its precious, yet innocent, son. Notice the cub is staring at every step the lion makes, however the lion is attentively focus on what is ahead. He is chary of a future that the cub has no idea is awaiting him.

The cub is looking at the lion as they sagaciously trot on the cover of this book. Notice closely, and you will discover that the cub is determined to strategically place his foot in stride with his father. In his attempt to keep the rhythm, the cub is mindful that he is fortunate to have the "King of the Jungle" as his example. He looks with great concentration, because he catches a glimpse of who he shall become. While gazing at this ferocious, muscular, and protruding stature of confidence, there, he sees himself.

At the same time, the lion is looking at the cub in his trepidation, apprehension, and attempting to balance it with adoration. The lion has lived a life that only the cub can imagine. His life-changing experiences are mysterious to the cub. He knows and understands what it will cost the cub to become a lion, while the cub is totally oblivious to the sacrifices that are demanded to become what he sees.

The lion sees, in the cub, himself in rewind, at the same moment, the cub sees, in the lion, himself in fast-forward.

This primer will serve as a constant catalyst by articulating the necessary steps to reach your full potential. Whether you are the lion or the cub, "Groomed for Greatness" will challenge you to strive to become the best you possible. It will provide both philosophical and pragmatic undertones for daily application. This project was intentionally designed to develop an appetite for greatness…I am not apologetic for that.

Just as the cub caught glimpses of greatness while watching the lion, you too will see yourself totally different while reading, studying, and completing the assignments found within this book. The life lessons that are contained here will aide you in "keeping the rhythm required to reach Greatness." One of the most disappointing confirmations of life is to have proficiencies that are hijacked by one's distorted proclivities.

Are you ready?

Because, you're next to be… Groomed for Greatness.

Introduction
You are Great, Now Believe It and Prove It Daily!

For the past 28 years I have been privileged to understand and operate in my purpose. Purpose is defined as the "reason for which something is done or created or for which something exists." The mission, mandate and meaning of life, as I describe it, is proven by one's purpose for living, fulfillment, and ultimate success. It provides motivation for the mission in life that you are to accomplish, maneuvering for each mandate you are confronted with, and the means for every situation you are to master. Everything was created for a purpose. Nothing was ever made, constructed, designed and developed without, first, an expected, anticipated, and attainable goal in mind. Just think about everything that is around you. It is serving a purpose. The chair, table, and even the rug they are situated on, is serving a purpose. This quote on purpose has the most profundity to me, "The greatest tragedy in life is not death, but life without a reason. It is dangerous to be alive and not know why you were given life"- Dr. Myles Munroe (In Pursuit of Purpose).

While writing this, I was sitting on an airplane taxiing to the runway to takeoff. My then 12 year old son, Kristian and I were in deep dialogue about the functions of this Airbus A320 jet. He is fascinated with the mechanical operations of such a huge aircraft from the small cockpit. How is it that a jumbo-jet that weighs over 170,000 pounds, is literally controlled by a throttle and small instruments? I was explaining to him how every part of this machine works in harmony for one goal. If the plane had no wings, we could not fly and without correct tires, we could not taxi properly. Without an engine, we would not travel at the speed needed to propel us into the air and maintain altitude. I reminded him that even with all of the proper mechanics in place, without a pilot and flight crew the plane still could not move. It was created with this purpose in mind.

We discussed the importance of the people on the plane as well as those outside of it. The grounds crew serves a viable purpose as well. If they were not operating in their purpose, then the plane would be grounded. Although the mechanical parts were all functioning, and the pilot and flight crew were in place, the grounds crew guided the aircraft and provided eyes for blind spots. Everything, as minute as it may seem, has purpose. Despite how you feel, your life has purpose.

For some, this process is simple, but for countless others, it is frustrating and difficult. It is rewarding to understand why you were born. It is fulfilling to hone in skills that will sharpen the discovery of why you were created at this time in history and not at another. There's satisfaction in waking up every day, working toward an expected accomplishment and achievement.

But, perhaps you are reading this 'primer' right now saying, "Well that is certainly not me because I am disappointed. My constant companions are the results of failed opportunities in my life. The same mediocrity meets me daily." Perhaps you are successful, but not satisfied. This would be a fantastic life for someone else, but not for you. Maybe struggle seems to remain a constant companion and the reoccurring question- "How long?" haunts you each moment.

This 'primer' is purposed to serve as the pilot and ground crew for the Airbus A320, to guide you from the gate of your departure, as you taxi to your designated runway for takeoff into your purpose. It will provide practical assessments that will assist you in determining, first, what you are not supposed to do, and cause what you should do to become visible. This "primer's purpose" is to alert you of the attitude needed to ascertain the desired goal for which you were born and created. The journey continues as you develop the basis for accountability, and agendas that will prepare you for how to deal with your adversities.

It is from your adversities that you discover the affirmation that they provide on your way to achievement. When these principles are applied, you will reach a cruising altitude in life that brings accomplishment. It will also prepare you for how to handle sudden turbulence, which I am sure you will encounter along the journey. Now to enjoy the flight that is your life. Trusting the training that you have been given, and the life lessons deposited on purpose that you are unaware of.

The two, training and life lessons, speak to your passion. After cruising, you will discovery that- "Passion is the fuel that allows your purpose to move."

Let's go, enjoy the ride of a lifetime while being "Groomed for Greatness."

Assessments

> "It's hard to be a diamond in a rhinestone world." — Dolly Parton

The Queen of Country Music was spot on with the aforementioned statement. Many a people have lived unfilled lives because they have mastered being something that they are not; exhausting great energy to mask the misery of falling short of what you were never created, intended to be. "Spending money or resources that you really do not have, on things you really cannot afford, to impress people mostly that we do not even admire." This has become the pattern of life chosen by so many people. I simply call it "Living a Diamond life on a Rhinestone budget." How you see yourself is important to proper alignment with your purpose. Assessment is defined as action or instance of appraisal. It is the opinion on the nature, character, or quality of something. The scales of self-appraisal will reveal significant data to guide you along this process. This analysis, if used properly, will become invaluable in the pursuit of your purpose. There is nothing more damaging than to view yourself as a diamond, but you are really a rhinestone. It was Brian Molko who once said, "Imitation is the highest form of flattery, but clones kind of get it wrong because we are promoting individuality and being proud of being yourself." I must admit that after reading the entire quote from Brian Molko, my appreciation of it has greater value.

Do you place more emphasis on the quality of life against quantity of it? Are you eagerly utilizing time to promote one at the others expense? Or, are you seeking the balance of both? Life is all about learning from others, but when I allow the quality traits that one possesses to overshadow my own, I have committed character suicide. Character suicide is when I eliminate personal talents, gifts, and other factors that comprise qualitative data about myself to become as someone else more revered. It is okay to be you. To experience life with the talents, tools, and gifts that you possess. Never underestimate yourself.

You are more powerful than you would believe or even imagine. At this very moment you possess some things that no one else on this planet has. Now, that makes you invaluable as you pursue your purpose. It is not until you relate and receive this that you can begin to unearth what you possess. When we lock ourselves out of the realm of possibilities, we then imprison ourselves from ever becoming what we were destined to be. You are destined to be so much the more…to live and dream and see those dreams become your reality. In life we can count our failures, and count on our failures I might add, to the point that we sabotage our own success. I will explore this subject later in this primer. We are provided with powerful possibilities daily, but we must choose to receive them in order for the possibilities to become revelation to us.

It is quite simple. Every day that I am alive, I should commit to pursuing and possessing everything that I can to propel me into my purpose for living. At best when I am not, my life is being wasted.

The polar opposite is to become underappreciated; those who know that you are a diamond, but value you only as a rhinestone. While it is important to appreciate how you see yourself, it is equally important that you understand how others critique you. Allow it to work for you and not against you. If your assessment of yourself is accurate, then prepare yourself for those who will purposely try to change you or the assessment. I would rather know that if, at best, I am a rhinestone, I do not need to be a diamond. In doing so, I have developed a true assessment of myself. That is who I am and I am okay with that. It is then that I am freed to express myself without fear of imitating something I will never be. It will allows you to view both strengths and weaknesses. They are both needed, because in life you will surmise that what makes you strong is derived from your weakness. Equally as important comparably, what makes you weak is from a lack appreciation of your strengths. Understanding is a key component here.

A lawyer once told me, "You are undoubtedly great at what you do. It is obvious that you were created, design and fitted for the purpose in life you have. No one can convince me otherwise. The abilities you possess and the precision to utilize them is remarkable. But, know that you are only great in particular areas.

You are not great in every area." I could have immediately become outraged and disgruntled at his statement. I had to make a conscious decision at that very moment. It was whether to continue listening to learn or complete ignore the remainder of the conversation. He continued as I listened to the incisiveness of his statement, "You must find others who are great at what you are not, and invite them to partner with you." By gaining relationships with others who have expertise in areas you do not, never makes you weak, but totally the opposite. Partnering with others to invest where you lack is a sound investment that reaps lifetime rewards. The simplicity of the statement almost caused me to under-value it. But, after pondering it, I admitted to this lawyer turned friend, that he was absolutely correct. In my own personal assessment, I had just gained several new principles. I will share them with you now.

5 Keys to Unlocking Your True Assessment

1. Remember, it is okay not to be great at everything.
2. Just Strive to be great in the areas I have discovered greatness in.
3. Realize that my next decision can limited me or release great potential in my life.
4. Accept that honesty hurts, but I heal as I grow.
5. The transformation of relationship. Complete thought?

Key # 1- It's okay not to be great in everything.

The veracity of this statement will shoulder the struggles of your life with undeniable strength. It provides a sense of clarity that allows perception of purpose to become vivid. The release of pressure added by attempting to live up to un-achievable goals will prove fruitful. This key enables you to stop focusing on deterrents and distractions. Life is filled with them and they will circumvent your progression. It is here you will locate & unlock the **door of discovery**. What are your talents, gifts, and abilities? We are all graced with some measure of them all each. The process of find these talents, gifts, and abilities will unlock for you the potential to operate in your purpose. Scan your entire life; what have you gravitated to and has interested you the most? It is hidden in this research that you will soon discover the meaning of life. I attended high school with a young man who desired to join the football team. He was not the most athletic or skilled player, but his determination to make the team was undeniable. He attended every practice. He was on time, but most of the passes thrown to him, he dropped. While running lapse, he would always finish last. He could not dominate on defense nor was he explosive on offense. By all standards he should not make the team. On the final day of try-outs, members of our team were puzzled to learn that in spite of all of his limitations and restrictions, he was on the team.

After a brief conversation with him, our coach made a statement that has remained a part of my life. He said that, in life we are not all destined to be great football players, but we can all become great people. His goal was to ensure that we all had the potential to become great in whatever area in life was calling us. It was through that lesson I learned that you will not be great in everything, but if dedicated, you will be great in something.

As elementary as it sounds, take two sheets of paper and list what you can do on one and what you cannot do on the other. This could take seconds, hours, days, weeks, and even months. But, after you list them, do not concentrate on what you cannot do well, as a matter of fact, file the list of things you cannot do. Make the list of potential areas of greatness your life marker to assist in your pursuit to the path of purpose.

Key # 2- Just Strive to be great in the areas you have discovered greatness in.

Now, that we have used Key #1 to locate & unlock the **door of discovery**, let us move to the next one. The next key to unlocking your true assessment is to strive to be great in the area(s) you have discovered greatness in. Now that you have an targeted your purpose, you need to use this key to unlock the **door of diligence**. Discovery provided a list of areas you are great in.

First, *celebrate* each of them. It is not as important as "how" many things are listed, as much as "what" is listed. Each of these designated areas have extraordinary potential in your being "Groomed for Greatness." Secondly, *concentrate* on each of the areas listed. Give diligent, careful and persistent work or effort to your itemized list of greatness. Herein lies the blueprint, if you will, for the success you have always desired and dreamed of. Do not minimize this list; it will become a life changing agent for you. From this list you should, thirdly, *cultivate* your areas of greatness. Strategically locate people and places that influence your areas of greatness. This will allow you to gain the insight and inspiration needed to bring your areas alive. A unique way to develop your areas of greatness is to serve others with them. In its most general form, humanitarianism is an ethic of kindness, benevolence and sympathy extended universally and impartially to all human beings. By using what you have to impact the lives of others is so rewarding. As absurd as it probably sounds to some, it is the litmus test for your pursuit of life's purpose.

Key # 3- Your My next decision can limited me or release great potential in my life.

We now find ourselves now at the **door of directives**. "Everything you do is a result of a decision." This is the mantra of World Wrestling Champion and successful entrepreneur, Leo Frincu, who .He came to the United States 10 years ago with $10 on his pocket and knowing only 4 words of English.

Combining his work ethic, knowledge, and adherence to discipline, Leo found a way to share his passion for athleticism and personal growth with people of all ages and walks of life. *RESULTS STUDIO* and *LeoFrincu.com* became the embodiment of Leo's burning desire to contribute to the community by enabling people to overcome personal adversity and reach their best potential. Start living life with intentions. The list that you have developed should serve as a guide while being groomed. The next decisions you make should not be haphazard, but methodical. This is ***powerful*** in your pursuit of purpose. Making a wrong decisions will delay your destination. I did not say mistakes, because we are all destined to make them, but making key decisions is essential.

The decision to complete this book was key. Your next decision is absolutely necessary for your purpose to have sustainability. What decisions should you make now that will affect you positively in the future? Guard your greatness with reinforcing the walls of your confidence. Do not allow doubt to become the silent partner to remove the building blocks you have worked to properly place in the stairway to your success. Also, in conjunction with the power, promptness is a major component in decision making. The "what" of our decisions is important as well as the "when" the promptness. While doubt will certainly cripple your decisions in life, it is delay that will question the credibility of it.

Napoleon Hill - "Promptness of decision is a very important factor in the attainment of a pleasing personality, and it is a very prominent trait in all successful persons. It is a habit which can be acquired through self-discipline. Promptness of decision develops as a result of a confident, constructive, sure and progressive positive mental attitude. It is closely related, as you will readily perceive, to definiteness of purpose, the starting point of all achievement." Making the right and timely decisions are significant, start today to ensure your tomorrow's are fulfilling.

Key #4- Honesty hurts, but you I heal as you I grow.

The question: "Why does the best advice seemingly hurt you the most?" was posed to me during a Q&A period after a seminar I conducted. In my own unique and eccentric way, I pulled from different areas of expertise until I remembered a quote by Winston Churchill, "Criticism may not be agreeable, but it is necessary. It fulfills the same function as pain in the human body. It calls attention to an unhealthy state of things." I believe that the pursuit of purpose is noteworthy, but the partners you trust to travel with along the way is paramount as well. Everyone needs someone in their lives life who will tell them the truth; a realist for the life we envision. In a later chapter, I will define that we all need someone in our lives life we can tell the truth to, but we certainly need someone to relate truth to us. Honesty is the foundation for futures success. It improves the spirit of fairness and straightforwardness in our conduct.

It authenticates the steps of sincerity we make daily. You must be honest with yourself and others and about your motives and actions. I would rather someone hurt me with the truth than to protect me with a lie. It will surely hurt, but I can heal as I grow.

Constructing a reality on a foundation of lies will not provide the structural assurance to build anything of substance or stability. The bible states in First Peter chapter 4 and verse 8; "Love hides a multitude of faults...." it does not state that it eradicates and lies about them. The truth is the fuel for the journey you will need to arrive at your destination. Remember that when someone relates truth to you, receive it. There are a plethora of paths after truth is related to us that we can choose, but you must just receive it. The process of healing is a sign of maturity. It is also is indicative that the pain during the process was not greater than the person or what was being produced in the process. Your survival is evidence that you possessed confidence.

 **Key #5- The transformation of relationship.**

Awaken intuition, attune to feelings, apply life-wisdom, practice the artful use of humor...transform the relationship with yourself. Relinquish old patterns, come home to your true self, speak authentically, listen from the heart, and discover the joy of co-creating relationships. This is a recipe for creating transforming relationships. Karen Bonnell has over 25 years of experience working with individuals, couples, and families facing transition, loss, stress and change.

How can transforming relationships help in my pursuit of purpose? Well, as you define the path of purpose that life has for you, you will then gravitate to people of like purpose or those who are in need of the purpose you were created for. This key literally brings us full circle.

The first two keys instructed you to make a list of strengths and weaknesses and to define the strengths as your areas of greatness. The second key challenged you to apply those areas of greatness to servitude and humanitarian efforts. The power of relationships will "Groom your Greatness" and supply longevity that is priceless. Relationships have the proficiency to illuminate the best in all of us. Some of the greatest areas of my life are built on relationships that have sustained me through the test of time. The relationship with my wife, son & daughter, family, colleagues and peers all have different roles and responsibilities, but each plays an undeniable function in my being "Groomed for Greatness." The third key reminds you that- My next decision can limited me or release great potential. The fourth key is honesty hurts, but you I heal as you I grow, and the fifth key is the transformation of relationships that are important for success. The invaluable deposits and withdrawals from these transforming relationships speak volumes to my success and serve as the coping agent during the defeats. You are only as strong as the relationships you have developed, and as weak as the ones you have not. To be great you must research every relationship you presently have, as well as potential ones in the future.

Meeting the right person at the wrong time will allow you to make investments that reap huge dividends in the future. But, meeting the wrong person at the right time could cost you more than you are willing to pay. Transform every relationship into seeds of greatness to plant into your life and harvest at the time you need them most. Now that we completed the *5 Keys to Unlocking Your True Assessment*, we are prepared to move to the next stop on the path to purpose... **Attitude**!

The Cultural Transformation Tools consist of a series of assessment instruments that map the values of individuals and groups to the Seven Levels of Consciousness model.

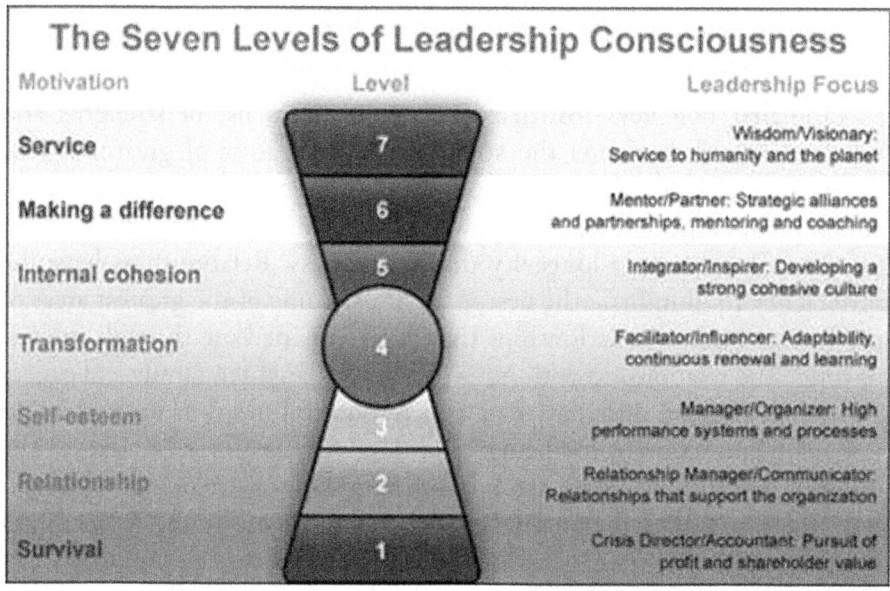

ATTITUDE

"When you're good at something, you'll tell everyone. When you're great at something, they will tell you." — Walter Payton

What is Attitude? Attitude is a mental position relative to a way of thinking or being; a leaning toward that which you believe. A positive attitude is, therefore, the inclination to generally be in an optimistic, hopeful state of mind. I agree with John C. Maxwell in his book, "The Difference Maker- Making Your Attitude Your Greatest Asset", when he stated that attitude is not everything, but it is the one thing that can make a difference in your life. The *Power of a Positive Attitude* is a major element in being "Groomed for Greatness." Your attitude has the ability to open and close doors for you. I have witnessed the most gifted and talented people miss tremendous opportunities because their attitude limited them. Their attitude turned on the talent they possessed and major doors were shut right in front of them. Your attitude is the thermostat that will gauge the climate of circumstances around you. The key to greatness is exemplified in the words graced atop this page by one of the greatest "pure" athletes to ever play football, Mr. Walter Payton. He was an American football running back who played for the Chicago Bears of the National Football League (NFL) for thirteen seasons. Despite his passing in 1999, Payton's off-season workouts are still spoken of regularly.

Those who played with him were amazed at his work ethic off the field. His nickname was simply, "Sweetness." His gifts, talents, and abilities set records that took years to eclipse. His presence has placed a stamp on humanity like none other. It is true, when you are good at something, you inform people about it. But, when you are great, they will inform you! I have often told those I have been privileged to mentor over the years that we all have talent(s), but gift(s) are rare.

Talent will only bless yourself, but a gift will bless others. Because you are being "Groomed for Greatness," you can never be settled to being talented. Transform those talents into gifts that will speak about you when you are no longer around.

The gift of greatness is harnessed with a positive humbling attitude. Very early in life and ministry, I was told by my seniors that if I remained humbled, there would never be a limit to my potential. I believe that to this very day. Your attitude breathes life into your character and feeds your integrity. Character and integrity are juxtaposed without the right attitude. It is said that character is who we are when we are all alone. Well, it's the attitude that keeps your character company during the darkness of time. Integrity is the adherence to moral and ethical principles; soundness of moral character; honesty. Well Attitude is the consciousness that speaks to integrity in her most trying hour. Attitude is not a position taken, but a lifestyle lived. The right attitude plus giftedness is a remarkable combination.

So, how should I construct the proper attitude that perpetuates greatness in my life? The answers to the following questions will equip you with the necessary tools to build an Attitude that Makes the Difference.

What Attitude is driving you presently?

What Attitude or mindset have you chosen to subscribe to?

Does your Attitude or mindset need a makeover?

Are you controlled by a Positive or Polluted Attitude?

The answers to each of these questions should be carefully considered. You must process each of them and answers with conviction and honesty. The adjustment of one's attitude is not a crime, but a sign of true maturity. How you answer each of these questions will allow you to draw closer to the destination of greatness you desire.

What Attitude is driving you presently?

The attitude you presently possess will need to be inspected. You must ask yourself this question, Can the attitude I possess survive when success or better comes? Whatever drives you will ultimately consume you. Is your attitude driven by monetary or financial attainment? Is it driven by personally being popular, and the importance of impressing others? Or to influence and impact on the lives of others?

Is yours an individual quest for purpose and life fulfillment? Whatever it is, it will need to be clearly defined, clearly because there are attitude roadblocks that will prevent you from achieving success. The answers to these questions will determine if you will arrive successfully or will need an "attitude tune up." Now, believe me, I understand that our attitudes differ from day to day, but just like driving, your objective is to remain in your lane. While others are swerving in and out of lanes with their own vicissitudes, you must remain focused. You must be cognizant of your speed and the speed limits. While others are pressing and pushing you to speed up in areas you are not prepared or desire to. You must watch out for road construction that will not deny your progress, but it could delay it. While the clutter and confusion of others in your office, family, and community vie to impede you on this journey. The Attitude that is driving you is important to success as well as survival. Don't allow the actions of others to dictate your decisions.

John Maxwell is quoted saying this about Attitude-

> *"Attitude, to me, is more important than education, than money, than circumstances, than failures, than successes, than what other people think or say or do. It is more important than appearance, giftedness or skill. It will make or break a company... a church... a home. The remarkable thing is we have a choice every day regarding the attitude we embrace for that day.*
>
> *We cannot change our past... we cannot change the fact that people act in a certain way. We cannot change the inevitable. The only thing we can do is play on the one string we have, and that is our attitude... I am convinced that life is 10 percent what happens to me and 90 percent how I react to it. And so it is with you... We are in charge of our attitudes."*

So, what you are allowing to drive your attitude is major. If life is in fact, 10 percent what happens to you and 90 percent how you react to it, you must take control of your attitude and demand the best it can produce today. Challenge yourself in new ways, standards, beliefs, and ideas. Remember, "Neither negative situations nor people can determine my attitude." Guard your attitude with all you have, because it is! An positive attitude permits me to feel better about myself, my circumstances, and those connected to me.

> "A positive attitude helps you cope more easily with the daily affairs of life. It brings optimism into your life, and makes it easier to avoid worries and negative thinking. If you adopt it as a way of life, it will bring constructive changes into your life, and makes them happier, brighter and more successful."

What Attitude or Mindset have you chosen to subscribe to?

The music you listen to, food you consume, and clothes you chose to wear all speak of the attitude you have chosen to subscribe to. "Persuasion is a basic form of social interaction," says Eric Knowles, Emeritus Professor of Psychology at the University of Arkansas in Fayetteville. "It is the way we build consensus and a common purpose." Take inventory of the music saved on your device, or what stations are presently programmed as favorites. Walk into your kitchen and look through the cabinets and refrigerator, all the contents speak volumes of who you are. The fade of clothes and trends of fashion is also a medium of expression. The name brand, or the lack thereof, will allow you to deduce what is most important to you. Persuasion is a powerful tool of influence. There is a psychological fact that people eat with their eyes. Think about the television programming late at night, with emphasis placed on selling you things that you would normally never become influenced by. The myriad of sales papers, coupons, and commercials concerning a huge sale on clothing, creates an appetite, if you will, of impulse purchasing. The use of actors and actresses, those whom appear famous or at the least known, star in the commercial with intentional marketing. New shoes, shirts, and jeans, that will offer you the opportunity to live vicariously through the person you admire from afar. Everything around us strategically and systematically speaks into our lives while vying for dominance for the day.

These battles are not limited to things, but even people wage war for commanding control of your attitude. Remember, your attitude is the compass of your purpose.

It will determine how and/or if you will accomplish the reason you are alive. It will assist you with the discovery of life's meaning. Your attitude serves as the plate that your purpose rests upon. Purpose is unfulfilled when attitude has the wrong subscription. Do you understand "Why the attitude you subscribe to is important" in the development of not "*who*" you are, but rather "*why*" you are? We spend meaningful moments attempting to impress people with what we have, over and against why we are who we are. I suggest to you today, the attitude of choice is too significant for you to allow someone else to decide for you. Remember, you are being "Groomed For Greatness." Your attitude will immensely affect your impact in this process. What factors daily determine how you see yourself? Should you avoid negative people who purposefully infect your attitude with the negativism they are poisoned with? I read a book entitled- "Good to Great." The author, Jim Collins, made a profound statement that assisted me in making this subscription for my attitude.

> *"Letting the wrong people stay around is unfair to all the right people, as they inevitably find themselves compensating for the inadequacies of the wrong people. Worse, it can drive away the best people. Strong performers are intrinsically motivated by performance, and when they see their efforts impeded by carrying extra weight, they eventually become frustrated."*

Your attitude is suffering because of the sacrifice of permitting the "wrong people" (those who are not good for you, and especially those who are not good to you) to remain. Don't allow temporary people to have a permanent space in your life.

It is proven that the "wrong people" will not only hurt you, but they will prevent people of purpose, the "right people" from staying with you.

Does Your Attitude Need A Makeover or Is It Flawless?

In an article published in GAIAM LIFE- "Your Guide To Better Living" by Kay Cross, Med, entitled "Extreme Attitude Makeover: 3 Steps to Attracting Success", it is stated that there are (3) three critical yet attainable steps in changing your attitude, have amazing power to make good things start happening, and give you're a life makeover. The (3) three steps are:

1. Develop Gratitude- Gratefulness promotes humility, stimulates your faith and promotes contentment. Dr. Cross concludes with this quote according to John Maxwell, author of The Winning Attitude, "Our attitude is the primary force that will determine whether we succeed or fail." In simple terms, your attitude will make or break you. The development of gratitude in your attitude is a winning combination. Grateful people are energetic and infectious even amongst those with negative views and demeanors.

2. Lead by Serving- The greatest leaders are those who serve. The way they accomplish that is by lifting everyone around them to greater heights and making them feel that they are an integral part of a team. Johann Wolfgang von Goethe states it perfectly: "Treat people as if they were what they ought to be and you help them to become what they are capable of being." I can personally attest to this quote. People love leaders who serve. The unique quality to serve, embodies the fact that true leadership is what you do, not where you sit. You will earn the respect of your followers, when you have an attitude of servitude.

3. Face Your Fears- John Maxwell says "fear is a stepping stone to growth." The fact is that we can use fear to our advantage. How can you conquer fear? One way is to reprogram your brain's responses to fear by intentionally putting yourself into new, uncomfortable situations. Another benchmark to set when facing your fears is to reflect on past situations. They can serve as the springboard to catapult you out of fear. Remember that fear thrives on the unknown, and undiscussed. The antidote to facing your fears is sometimes a simple conversation with someone you trust. Communication removes the walls of isolation where fear is most comfortable.

Are You Controlled by a Positive or Polluted Attitude?

Do you think you're a positive person? A positive mental attitude can improve your health, enhance your relationships, increase your chances of success, and add years to your life. The fact is, most people are bombarded by negativity each day. Sure, it's easy to cast blame by saying you're surrounded by negative people. The reality is, a lot of the negativity is self-inflicted... influenced by the company you keep and your personal perspective on life's realities. First and foremost, you must admit that whatever attitude you presently possess, is your choice. Although your surroundings are presently are positive or negative, the final decision to convert to one over against the other is yours to make. A positive attitude can boost your energy, heighten your inner strength, inspire others, and garner the fortitude to meet difficult challenges. According to research from the Mayo Clinic, positive thinking can increase your life span, decrease depression, reduce levels of distress, provide greater resistance to the common cold, offer better psychological and physical well-being, reduce the risk of death from cardiovascular disease, and enable you to cope better during hardships and times of stress.

Here are several ways to adopt a positive mental attitude:

- **Surround yourself with positive people.** Spend time with people who are positive, supportive, and who energize you. Remember, if you get too close to a drowning victim, he may take you down with him. Pick a positive person instead.

- **Be positive yourself.** If you don't want to be surrounded by negative people, what makes you think others do? Learn to master your own thoughts. For example: When you visualize a goal, it makes you more likely to take the actions necessary to reach it. Visualize yourself winning the race, getting the promotion, accepting the award, or landing the new account.

- **Control your negative thinking.** This can be accomplished in the following ways:

  ✓ See the glass as half full rather than half empty.

  ✓ Anticipate the best outcome.

  ✓ Stay the middle ground. Don't view everything in extremes — as either fantastic or a catastrophe. This will help you reduce your highs and lows.

  ✓ Accept that mistakes happen. Negative people blame themselves for every bad occurrence whether it was their fault or not. Don't let this be you.

  ✓ Consciously resist negative thinking. Be cognizant of and mentally avoid negative thinking. This will help you modify your behavior. Be nice to yourself. Unfortunately, some people say the meanest things to themselves. If you criticize yourself long enough, you'll start to believe it. This negativity can drag you down over time. It may be time to fire the critic and hire the advocate.

Groomed for Greatness will demand that your attitude have continuous adjustments and alignments. When we constantly check our attitudes we can determine when those necessary adjustments and alignments are needed. Don't travel life's highway out of alignment because of your attitude. Get it adjusted, it makes the ride much safer and smoother.

WHAT WE THINK, WE ARE..

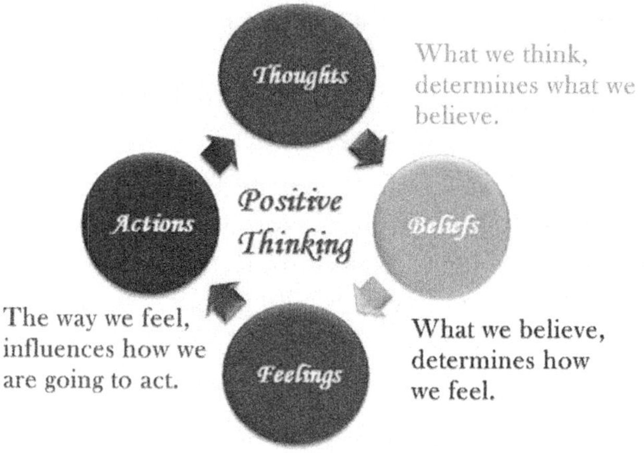
Thoughts
What we think, determines what we believe.
Beliefs
What we believe, determines how we feel.
Feelings
The way we feel, influences how we are going to act.
Actions
Positive Thinking

You can't live a positive life with negative mind.

ACCOUNTABILITY

"When your persona gets bigger than your person, then who you have become will kill who you are"- Bishop T.D. Jakes

Accountability is defined by Merriam Webster as: An obligation or willingness to accept responsibility or to account for one's actions. How much of your success would you say is up to you—your choices, your actions, your behaviors—versus outside conditions? In an article, published on the website of the AMA- American Management Association, by Linda Galindo entitled: "No Excuses: Being Accountable for Your Own Success" states:

If your mind-set is that you're at least 85% responsible for your success—and that just 15% depends on the way the wind blows—you'll likely be successful. If you blame your problems and failures—big or small, personal or professional—on other people, circumstances beyond your control, or just plain bad luck, you may be doomed to fail. The good news? Accountability is not just a mind-set—it's also a skill-set that everyone can learn. It may not be as easy as one,-two,-three, but it is a three-step process.

Responsibility	Self- Improvement	Personal Accountability
A. Be Responsible	A. Manage Expectations	A. Tell the Truth
B. Recognize Your Power	B. Take Back Your Time	B. Police Yourself
C. Deal With What Is	C. Sing Your Own Praise	C. Look to Yourself First

Accountability will always call for you to have (3) three individuals in your life. These persons will help to facilitate, assist with what frustrates, and sometimes fascinate you. They are irreplaceable and indispensable. Their roles are defined and developed over the maturation of your life, although they probably will never know each other. The success of each is to maintain integrity in the lane in which they have been assigned. You must permit them to remain in their respective roles, and not give in to the pressure to make one of them a "one stop shop." The mantra for each of them is "Stay in Your Lane", at all times, and at all cost. It will astonish you that, while placing these (3) persons in your own life, you will see the need to be placed in someone else's life for reciprocal reasons.

Now, let's meet them:

The Mentor	*The Mirror*	*The Mentee*
"Will help you to facilitate"	"Will assist with what frustrates"	"Will sometimes fascinate"

The University of Washington- Human Resources webpage has an interesting article on the subject of Career Development; it is the "Mentee Guide"- Keys to a Successful Mentor/Mentee Relationship. The emphasis is placed upon understanding the importance of Partnering and Mentoring. The two are often intertwined in conversation and discussion. While both partnering and mentoring are not synonymous, they are harmonious. This is significant in maintaining the integrity, previously mentioned, and lane assignment. Jooli Atkins, BCS Fellow and Managing Director of Matrix Forty-two, discusses the differences between partnering and mentoring, explaining how both kinds of programs can improve business productivity.

"An understanding of the history of mentoring is something that I believe adds tremendously to the skills of a good mentor."

Questions that always surface are 'What are the differences between partnering and mentoring?' and 'When would you use either one?' Therefore to better understand how partnering and mentoring can demonstrate the business value we need to understand at the differences between the two. For a partner, the task at hand is most important. The partner has to help the person learn the requisite attitude, behavior and skills needed to perform the job successfully within the agreed success parameters. The task is therefore well defined and the conversation happens with a clear focus and specific timelines. Mentoring focuses on the individual and the conversation transcends more broadly into general work life. This means the interaction can be more philosophical, more focused on attitudes and behaviors than on specific skills.

Partnering is a relationship, frequently between two people, in which each has equal status and a certain independence, but also implicit or formal obligations to the other.

Mentoring is often thought of as a partnership largely because there are obligations, implicit or otherwise, that each party takes on. One key to a successful mentee/mentor relationship is to be aware of your obligations and take them seriously.

Questions to ponder:

What obligations might you take on as a mentee? What challenges might arise for you in relation to these obligations? How can you partner with your mentor to meet your obligations to him or her?

Inviting a Mentor's Assistance

Because mentoring is most often a voluntary activity on the part of the mentor, it is important that you think carefully and intentionally about what you want from a mentor's assistance. A mentor's responsibility to the mentee is invaluable, but costly. The relationship being built is one of a lifetime commitment. It should never be taken for granted and always cherished. The mentor is giving more than just advice and guidance, but rather pieces of their own personal life experiences. Finding the right mentor is just as important as locating the right mentee. Every person who has ever reached the plateau of success they desired, had a mentor. They had someone who supplied them with what no one else could or would. The essentials of their relationship are rarely ever public, but thrive in privacy. A mentor is critical if you are serious about achieving life's goals and benchmarks.

No mentor desires to pour good information, valuable life experiences, and priceless moments of time that can never be replenished, into an unappreciative and unproductive vessel.

Most mentors live in silence due to the fact they dare not waste time and talent with the insignificant. Mentors have this innate ability to see more in the mentee than they can perceive about themselves. The mentor seeks to cultivate the mentee, to cause greatness to surface in them. The objective of the mentor is to challenge the mentee to dig deeper than they thought they could dig, go farther than they thought they could go, and be more than they thought they could be. Mentors never work for compensation, although the mentee should, in all their power, do so in some capacity. The greatest reward that a mentee can give to a mentor is utilize what has been planted in them by their mentor. Mentee's must allow seeds to germinate and grow to produce the fruit that the mentor knew was there the entire time. Only mentors can see fruit on empty branches.

Accountability is major component in the relationship between mentor and mentee. I have made this statement to every mentee I was privileged to guide. As well as each person who has allowed me to share wisdom principles with them: "In life, always have someone you can tell the truth to. Even when you have lied to everyone else." For harmony to exist between mentor and mentee, lying cannot be tolerated.

What most mentors are looking for from a mentoring relationship is:
- A sense that they are helping someone achieve their goals and that they are making a difference in another person's life.
- An occasional "thank you" or acknowledgement of the assistance they are providing.
- An enjoyable relationship.

Mentees

Building Trust- A mentoring relationship is based on trust. As a mentee, you are placing a great deal of trust in your mentor to provide you with helpful guidance. At the same time, mentors are trusting that mentees will not take advantage of the relationship (e.g., wasting your mentor's time, repeating information not intended for others, asking for favors, inappropriately using the relationship). Building trust can take time; our behaviors can accelerate the time it takes. Give some thought about what behaviors can help you quickly establish trust with your mentor. The common denominator of accountability is trust; the ability to be open with someone at the expense of being embarrassed. Mentors never manipulate mentees.

There is a difference in serving and being a slave. To unlock the door of trust you will need to possess the right key.

The Necessary Keys for a Mentee/Mentor Relationship

- Mutual respect.
- Acceptance and flexibility.
- Honesty and direct communication.
- Preparation.
- Commitment.
- Some shared values.
- Trust.
- Willingness to work through obstacles.

Mentees should know that one of the most important tasks to perform in building and maintaining a productive relationship with a mentor is to be very clear with him or her about what you expect and need. Be very specific. The best relationships will fail if there are unstated needs and expectations that are not being met. It is impossible to meet needs that were not revealed. No mentor can meet all of your needs, and it is crucial to give a mentor the opportunity to clarify what need(s) the can be meet.

Ending the Relationship

It will become inevitably clear that you sense your needs no longer can be met by your mentor and therefore it's time to end the relationship. Ending the mentoring relationship well is important to your continued success - first impressions and last impressions are what we remember most about others. Make your last impression a positive one.

Mirror

The role of the person who serves in the capacity of a "mirror" to you is certainly different from the mentor and/or mentor. The mirror does not necessarily give advice each time. You are not obligated to mentor them, but this persons understands the frustrations you face. This person understands your convictions and feels comfortable sharing your most intimate situations. The person who serves as your mirror does not encourage you to climb the mountains you face, they are not atop the mountain cheering you on. But, they are climbing right beside you, struggling and succeeding the entire journey; mostly because they can identify personally or practically. The mirror brings encouragement when needed. This person has the innate ability to listen without always being interjecting. Your "mirror" is invaluable because they understand their role is not to guide the car you're in, but to ride with you and assist when you have lost your way on life's highway. The mirror is usually a best friend, or a longtime friend or companion.

This persons allows you to encourage them as well. They expect it from you as key components of the relationship you share. Do not confuse the roles of the relationship with your mirror. They should never compete nor complete, but rather compliment you. This person should celebrate and not tolerate you.

There are a number of things you can do to invite initial and ongoing interest from someone to serve as your mirror.

- Know what you need and want from the relationship.
- Have clearly-defined objectives.
- Identify problems you believe might be obstacles to you in reaching your objectives.
- Give thought to and be able to articulate how you think a mirror could assist you.
- Think about how you might reach your objectives with or without a mirror.
- Be purposeful and pleasant, and have challenging goals.
- Treat your mirror relationship with care; don't abuse it by asking for inappropriate favors or information, and don't take your mirror for granted.

The Big (3) Mentor, Mirror, and Mentee will always play a pivotal role at different stages and scenarios in your ascension in life to success. Make sure they all stay in their lane! Make sure you stay in the lane of accountability to each of them.

AGENDAS

> "When you are destined for greatness, it shows in everything you do.
>
> **Greatness becomes you!**
>
> **Lori Myers, 3 Off the Tee: Targeting Success**

A meeting without an agenda can prove fruitless and a waste of time. It can seemingly last forever, going on and on. Nothing is accomplished because decisions cannot be made. The main issues of importance are never properly addressed. The meeting is dominated by the same participants and then protested by silent participants. Most of all, key people seldom attend and the lack of follow up is frustrating. The purpose of an agenda is ensure some specifics. It is the difference in firing a shot gun or rifle with a scope. The shot gun will hit something, but does not guarantee the target. When a rifle is used, and a scope applied, the target can be focused on and the probability of hitting it is raised. Being "Groomed for Greatness" you will need a scope to hit the desired targets of success. Agendas curtail and critique. They serve as the much needed guardians against any possible distractions from what is demanding our attention. Agendas once set are the bedrocks and successfully guide you from benchmark to benchmark.

Agendas are set to build the following:

- ✓ Items of Importance- "What are germane to reaching our goals"
- ✓ Desired Outcome- "Signs and signals to alert that we have accomplished goals"

- ✓ Priority- "Deciding what and where it is placed is vital"
- ✓ Time- "Management will determine the success whether goals are met or not"
- ✓ Who- "Judgment call will either create harmony or tension"
- ✓ How- "Plan of action"

Each of us have routines/agendas we're generally unaware of that we follow daily. Our agendas or habits can become our best friend and our worst enemy.

What are the items of importance and Desired Outcomes you desire? Have you given Priority and Time consideration to your daily routine? The "Who" and "How" will remain lacking with no plan of action. Like most people, we all have tasks that need completion. Steven Pressfield, author of "The War Art: Break through the Blocks & Win Your Inner Creative Battle" gave a profound quote on priority. "The Principle of Priority states: (a) You must know the difference between what is urgent ad what is important and (b) You must do what is important first."

The Principle of Priority

This principle encompasses each of the (6) components listed above. Groomed for Greatness has a set of priorities that you should consider:

- ✓ **Priority eliminates confusion**. When you set priorities, it helps you focus. There is less difficulty in seeing what you should do and what your motivations are in doing it. Priority creates a more natural pull to the activities that you know will give you the life you desire.

- ✓ **Priority negates compromise**. It is hard to be out of sync with your priorities for any length of time. The priorities will always bring you back to the central behavior and action that is critical to success. You are more unwavering and dogmatic with your time and the way you go about making sure the important things get done.

- ✓ **Priority increases commitment**. Whatever you make priority that is values based, it is easier to have the commitment for that priority. The more you execute the priorities, the more momentum you develop for other growth tasks.

I read an interesting article in Forbes Magazine by Jennifer Cohen, entitled **"Do You Want to Change Your Life for the Better"** on September 11, 2013. She listed 7 Different Ways to Make It a Habit. Each of them were interconnected and underscored the principle of priority.

One of the greatest deterrents to living a better life is breaking old habits, routines, and life agendas. It is easier to remain the same and keep telling yourself, "I will change one day" or "It's just the way it is." But, even if it is what it is, it does not have to remain that way. The very fact that you're reading this, is proof that the flame of change has not gone out in you. The wind of expectation can still blow across the embers of your heart and spark change.

Charles Duhigg author of "The Power of Habit" has an interesting concept called Keystone Habits- the habit(s) you identify as the most important things you can change about your life. This is the first step to series of steps to changing who you are to who you want to become. The intrigue is mounting and now envision yourself better. To find out what your Keystone Habit(s) are ask yourself- What consistently gnaws at you? It is something simply that you do that want to eliminate or even something you do not and desire to start. Granted, it could possibly take you longer to locate yours than others, and that's alright too. The purpose is not to locate it quickly, but thoroughly.

No matter what your discovery uncovers, remember whatever Keystone Habit you choose, work on it one at a time. Please do not repeat the mistakes that others have made in trying to resolve all of their issues with one treatment. Those battling a terminal illness will tell you that you must commit with endurance. Interested? Let's get deeper.

The opening quote by Lori Myers, "When you are destined for greatness, it shows in everything you do, Greatness becomes you" is not just an afterthought, but it is painstakingly cause you to rethink your daily routine and life agenda. Perhaps greatness is no longer pursuing you because it has positioned itself in you. Greatness living in you drives everything you do, to become great. I have discovered Great People think Great thoughts, read/write Great Books, do Great things.

It becomes habitual for them. This in no way negates struggle in their lives, but Great people seemingly preserve, Greatly. Stop making excuses as to why you gravitate to greatness. I remember watching Michael Jordan in NBA Finals- June 11, 1997, and the commentators questioning is greatness to rise to the occasion. Would he take control of the game and place his team on his shoulders. Could he find the balance between being a triple threat; outstanding scorer, leader, and involving his teammates. On this particular night, Jordan had the flu and many even doubted he would play, not alone perform to his ability.

But, sure enough, he mustered the strength to not only play, but perform with greatness. His 38-points despite flu-like symptoms, secure the victory for the Chicago Bulls. It did come with a price though. You could easily detect during time outs, the chills as he wrapped himself in towels, covered his head frequently, seem totally exhausted, and yes even vomiting. But, when he took to the court, he played with greatness, because he had become it. It was undeniable by his worst critics.

Now, I hear you saying, I am no Michael Jordan. But, in reality you have excelled in areas due to the fact that the greatness you pursued had now possessed you. It provided you with a spark of hope and energy that you found deep down inside of you. Maybe it was not a jump shot, but how you jumped into character and left everyone spellbound at your ability to produce under pressure.

No it was not the winning free throw to win the game, but it was the free spirit you displayed when assisting others at your own expense. Picking people up never diminishes your greatness, but on the contrary, it allows it to be shone brighter. You did not breakaway on a fast break and amaze the crowd with a thundering dunk, but you slammed the presentation that sealed the deal for your organization. We are not obligated to be great where others are, we just have to be great where we are called to be great. The ideology of being great at numerous things is a fantasy. You are only responsible for the greatness in you, not in others.

The Principle of Responsibility

This principle removes the fault off of others and then place it solely on ourselves. The blame game has been in play since the beginning of time. It is convenient to force our idiosyncrasies (a mode of behavior or way of thought peculiar to an individual) upon others. To shift the weight of responsibility to someone else is a sign of immaturity. The Principle of Responsibility acknowledges that you understand and bear the full burden upon yourself.

It is within the dynamics of this principle we see:

✓ It's Life's Ethical Compass

An Ethical Compass is an internal device that begins to develop a core of strength and assurance, mental and physical, when the journey of life takes you into uncharted territory. It serves as a mental mechanism that will guide you, despite the darkness you face. It is there to assist you with an inner vision, when you are challenged with the decision that have blind spots. This compass is really comprised to develop interpersonal skills, social consciousness, and human values. It acts a blueprint to trust as travel the unfamiliar terrains of life. You can trust the compass, even when you cannot trust yourself.

It lives in solitude somewhere in the sanctuary of your own soul. The compass has a voice that only you can hear, but when it speaks, it provides the assurance that is need to overcome the fear you face. The compass will bring to your remembrance the values that helped to shape and mold you into who you really are. The morality code that governs your thoughts, even when we dare to lean in the direction of the strange, sadistic, and sullen. It is there to say to us, "Turn right here" or "Turn Left ahead" and sometimes "Keep going and do not give up." I have relied on the ethical compass buried deep inside of me all of my life. It has served as the only friend I could and wanted to hear from when crisis were attempting to choke the life out of me. It was vivid and vociferous, even when I was trying to talk myself out of what I felt and knew was right.

The compass helped me get back on the right path in pursuit of my purpose. The constant thoughts associated with being lost is not fun at all. I have battled my own inner revolution, when I was so confused. My mind was convincing me to do one thing, while my heart was convicting me to do another. I slammed on the brakes of life and cried out to the compass. The compass never wavered. It always reveal truth to me, especially in times when I did not desire it. It did not spare my feelings or even consider what my mind nor my heart was thinking. The compass did not tell me what I wanted to hear, but what I needed.

No matter how long you ignore it, the ethical compass remains active. Its voice could possibly become fatigued and frustrated over time, but the very moment you give it attention, life springs back into it. The subscription never expires or lapse. Listen to it and test it. Trust the ethical compass for small projects and pursuits. Believe what it is telling you. It has the best intentions for you.

✓ It Represents Our Values

The principle of responsibility not only provide life's ethical compass, but it also represents the balance of my values. Socrates was a classical Greek philosopher credited as one of the founders of Western philosophy. He is quoted having stated: "Not life, but good life, is to be chiefly valued.

While being "Groomed for Greatness" ask yourself this question(s) and answer honestly:

➢ What are your values?
➢ What set of values have you adopted?
➢ Do you know what your personal value system consist of?
➢ Have you created a personal life platform of values?

Your answers will provide the necessary data to accurately assess where you are and where you can go in life. We fly or fail based on these answers. Your Value System is a critical component that supports the principle of responsibility. It is a set of practical principles or ideas that stimulate and/or governs your behavior. It provides structure and purpose by assisting you in determining what is most meaningful and important to you. They are building blocks properly placed in you by parents, grandparents, friends, mentors, and personal assessment. Perhaps it is a series of life stories passed down through the generations. Those defining moments that cannot be eradicated or eroded by time. Maybe notes from a book you have read that awaken your inner beliefs and dreams. It could be statements from a speaker who aroused in you the core criteria needed for course of life you have chosen. Possibly the nod of confidence you needed to build your confidence that the right choice was made.

Your Value System supports what I call your personal life platform. During each election, voters are challenged to cast their vote of support. Candidates are selected, speeches are made, banners are hung and the campaign trails are decided, in every attempt to sway voters' to a particular person. This choice is often with the candidate that best presents a platform that speaks to the voters' values. No matter if it seems as trivial as an elementary class or even the President of the United States of America, we should vote on the basis of values described in the candidates' platform. A platform speaks to the "intentions" of the candidate.

But, your personal life platform speaks to your "convictions" and persuasions. The candidates "intentions" most often change after the election, then your personal "convictions" and values should remain solid. You must trust your values as the bedrock of your life's platform. It will inevitably answer the following questions about you:

1. **Who You Are?**
2. **What You Stand For?**
3. **What You Accept?**

Your loyalty to your Life's Platform will always lend the same answers to the questions above. It is when we disconnect from our value system, and abandon the principle of responsibility, that we make questionable choices.

The danger comes when we make those choices based on the need for instant gratification from a person or project. Whenever we feel have an insatiable appetite for the applause of people and from projects, we hold our value system hostage.

The ropes of irresponsibility wrap around the value of truth that is at the core of "Who You Are" and refuse to let you go. Those ropes will dedicate themselves to holding you from achieving your full potential.

The ropes know that over time they will weaken, but are committed to annoying you in the process. The ransom paid for the lack of morality binds **"What You Stand For"** and demands payment in full. Immorality does not accept partial payments, and even when full payment is received, cannot be trusted to release your values. Indifference comes to rob you of **"What You Accept"** because then and only then are you vulnerable. When indifference wearies your values of what is acceptable, we make the fatal transfer of making wrong right, and right wrong.

So you see it is important that you're Value System remain operable and fully functional. Any breakdown will result in our being tied with ropes of irresponsibility, while the ransom of immorality is negotiated, and we are robbed by indifference. Check your system and repair any dysfunction quickly. Make the necessary updates and downloads to ensure that you're system is properly functioning. Remind yourself of the series of stories passed down through the generations.

Listen again to the voice of your parents and grandparents recorded in your mind. Review the notes from the speech that sparked you're spirit to formulate the values you have. Re-read that book. Envision that nod of confidence you received that cemented the decision that has guided you.

The caution you give ignore today, is the price of peace you will pay later. Allow you Value System to protect life's greatest commodity, YOU!

Groomed for Greatest is designed to assist with appropriating the right adjustments to your agenda. Subtracting those distractions that persistently prevent you from obtaining your goals. Adding those details that makes the difference needed to move from "Good to Great" is in the details. Paying attention to the details are acute accessing the next level or dimension of success. The details reveal the motives of the matter. It also defines the character of the individual. Anyone who does not give particularly time to details will have to answer the steady stream of questions concerning longevity. A true mentor will not allow you to cut corners to have completion, but will demand that that you work on the details. My mother would often ask me to sweep the floor, rather tell me, and if I did it half-heartedly, she would without fail, call me back to repeat the process. I hear her building my Value System by saying, "If you take the time dedicated to doing it right the first time, I would not have to call you back." This value has remained an icon on any project I commit to.

It is also dedicated to applauding when the right agenda has been secured. Perhaps you have made the necessary adjustments and your life's agenda is working properly for you. We all enjoy life's confirmation for time to time. You should not live for confirmation in every instance of your life, because it will eliminate the ability to take some risk.

> Many experts will tell you that if it were not for taking a risk, they would not be who or where they are now. The right adjustments to your agenda will lend the confidence to make choices that pay off each time. The CEO of Facebook is quoted having said: "The biggest risk is not taking any risk... In a world that changing really quickly, the only strategy that is guaranteed to fail is not taking risks."
>
> - Mark Zuckerberg

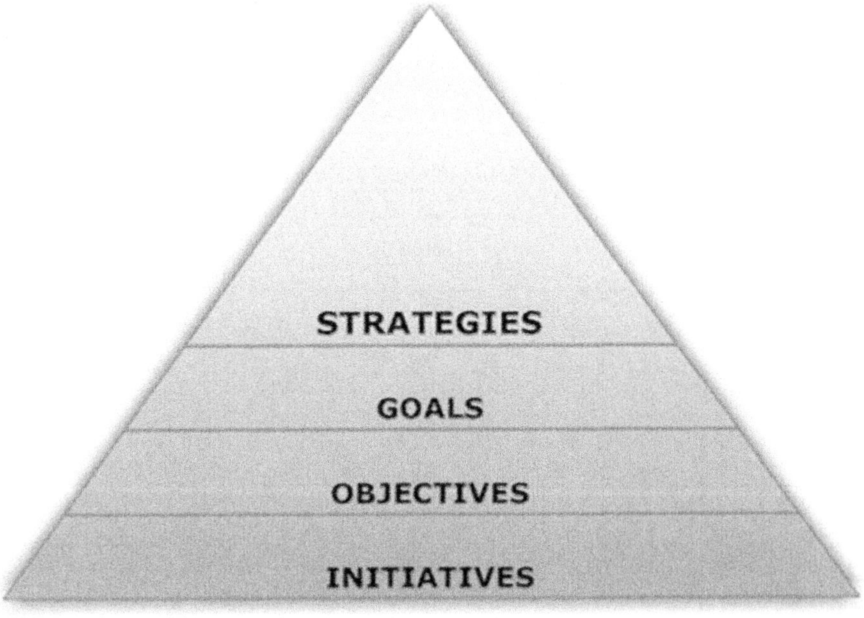
STRATEGIES
GOALS
OBJECTIVES
INITIATIVES

Traditional Model

Adversity

"Great spirits have always encountered violent opposition from mediocre minds"-Albert Einstein

Nelson Mandela personifies the quote above by Albert Einstein with grace. He spent 27 Years as a Political Prisoner. He became a leader among his fellow inmates, fighting for better treatment, better food and study privileges, earning his B.A. while imprisoned through a correspondence course. He also became a symbol of hope and anti-apartheid resistance for his entire country. While behind bars, he continued to build his reputation as a political leader, refusing to compromise his beliefs to gain freedom, and upon his release, he led negotiations that resulted in the democracy he had always fought for. He was elected president of South Africa and received more than 250 awards, including the Nobel Peace Prize. His funeral was a global event.

He could have decided to lie low, give in, and let those 27 years sap his motivation and his influence. It would have been easy enough. But he didn't.

Adversity is the ingredient in life we must all use whether we like it or not. We do not have the option of using a sprinkle here or there in certain dishes, but it is mandated for consumption.

No one will ever have the vantage point of saying that I maneuvered life's obstacle course and managed to complete it without adversity. It is part of life. For some it will make them bitter, while others better. Which one do you live with? Havelock Ellis wrote, "Pain and death are part of life. To reject them is to reject life itself."

The alchemy of adversity is best seen in an article published in Time Magazine on December 6, 2013 by Alex Perry of Cape Town, South Africa where he stated;

"Desmond Tutu once told me he believed prison was the making of Nelson Mandela. "I often surprise people when I say this," he said. "Suffering can lead to bitterness. But suffering is also the infallible test of the openness of a leader, of their selflessness." When Mandela had gone to jail, he had been "one of the most angry" said Tutu. "The suffering of those 27 years helped to purify him and grow the magnanimity that would become his hallmark." Jail helped Mandela learn how to make enemies into friends, said Tutu. It also gave him an unassailable credibility. "When you speak of forgiveness, 27 years in prison sets you up very nicely," he said.

Adversity will walk in the life of every individual without knocking or seeking permission to enter. It will make no apologies for the lateness of the hour when showing up and none for staying into the wee hours of the next morning.

Adversity will take a seat at the dinner table, in your mind, while great intensive conversation is taking place. It will climb right in your bed and seduce your dreams into nightmares. Invades your shower, and sits beside you in the Jacuzzi, while you are trying to relax. It is truly rude at times. Strangely, adversity rarely travels alone, he brings comrades name **suffering**, **hardship**, **difficulty**, **misfortune**, and **hard times**. Their objective is threaten every thought you have and ravish the inclinations of hope. To be honest, they are very experienced and professional in their operation. They are skilled and perfectionist. The completion of the job is when depression, disillusion, and death come to collect what is left.

But, there is an antidote for adversity. Every challenge and every difficulty we successfully confront in life serves to strengthen our will, confidence and ability to conquer future obstacles. Herodotus, the Greek philosopher, said, "Adversity has the effect of drawing out strength and qualities of a man that would have lain dormant in its absence." When adversity is observed correctly, then you can combat the company that it brings. Be aware of, and accept that adversity is inevitable in life. As has already been pointed out, adversity is part of life. To avoid or resist it will only make it persist. Everywhere you look in the world there is unmistakable struggle. There are floods, tsunamis, wars, and calamities of all types. Even within your own circle of family and friends there is death, loss and tragedy. Although pain is inevitable, suffering is optional. So what do you do?

People often misread an event or circumstance as an adversity or setback. The problem is that, we tend to judge events on the basis of their immediate impact. But, as life repeatedly teaches us, the long-term consequences of an action can be quite different from what we initially observe. The bad is superficial and obvious; the good often takes investigation and long-term observation. It's important to recognize that the true result of an event may take a long period of time to come to fruition. Thus, misfortune and setbacks are frequently nothing more than illusions, which is why we so often fail to connect the long-term benefits to the seemingly negative situation that confronts us.

Determine adversities pattern. What are the triggers identify that adversity is imminent? Anyone who is being **"Groomed for Greatness"** should be aware that a major deterrent is adversity. But, when greatness resides in you, adversity will cause inner strength to surface.

Take the situation at face value. Do not fall prey to imagining that the situation is worse than what it really is. Stop overthinking the circumstance, and do not cripple yourself with your own conversation. Adversity has a unique capability of using your words against you. It will also tempt you to poison other people because you are suffering. People make some of the most insensitive statements when stress and fatigue have flabbergasted them.

The old nursery rhyme states: "Sticks and stones may break my bones, but words will never hurt me." The nursery rhyme is fantasy exaggerated. Words can hurt you, and even kill you. Your words have the capacity to place irreparable and collateral damage in someone's life. Adversity has a pattern that is the key to observing how it functions and eliminate it prior to it setting mines throughout your field.

For some its stress at work (deadlines, schedule, co-workers, and even the boss) or parenting (the struggle with inconsistency, behavioral issues, lack of communication) and others it's financial and mounting debt. What triggers one does not necessarily affect someone else. The loss of a love one, while for another it is the birth of a new baby. Adversity is non bias. It does not have a preference of ethnicity, creed, or color. Your socio-economic status will not alter adversity. It invades the poorest family to the wealthiest. It visits the ghettos, public housing complexes, and the slums. Adversity also knows where the middle-class families dwells as well as the code to gated communities and access to mansions. It is the shared common denominator of human existence. But when its pattern is discovery, then identify the person who triggers adversity. Relationships, even the best of them, can have the propensity to add stress and tension to your life. Dating and intimacy increase the levels that one can experience. There are relationships that are non-sexual, have no intimacy and/or attraction factor involve, and still bring stress and tension in for the form of adversity. An employment relationship can surely bring similar symptoms.

It can become so unbearable that a person will choose to terminate the employment, or even the employer. In researching data for this section, I read a very intriguing article: "Types of Relationships" – This typology was devised by Carmen Lynch, M.F.C.C., a couples and family therapist in private practice on the Peninsula south of San Francisco. Victor Daniels, Professor of Psychology at Sonoma State University took notes on a talk in which she described it, added two categories and a few additional ideas, and wrote it down in the form in which it is presented here. The article referenced several types of relationships;

THE DOMINANT/COLLATERAL PATTERNS

1. SURVIVAL RELATIONSHIPS. These exist when partners feel like they can't make it on their own. The choice of a partner tends to be undiscriminating, made out of emotional starvation; almost anyone available will do. This involves relating at its most basic: "Without you I am nothing; with you I am something."

2. VALIDATION RELATIONSHIPS. A person may seek another's validation of his or her physical attractiveness, intellect, social status, sexuality, wealth, or some other attribute. Sex and money are especially common validators.

3. SCRIPTED RELATIONSHIPS. This common pattern often begins when the partners both are just out of high school or college. They seem to be "the perfect pair," fitting almost all the external criteria of what an appropriate mate should be like.

4. ACCEPTANCE RELATIONSHIPS. This is what many of us thought we were getting into when we entered a relationship, including many people in the three categories above. In an acceptance relationship we trust, support and enjoy each other. And within broad limits, we are ourselves. But each of us has a good sense of which aspects of our personal selves lie outside those limits. I find ways to restrain myself from pushing those limits that erode your trust, strain your enjoyment, and weaken your support for me.

5. INDIVIDUATION-ASSERTION RELATIONSHIPS. These relationships are based on the assertion of each person's wants and needs, and on respect for the other person's process of personal growth. Often they are focused on partners' struggles with what is missing or lacking in terms of self-discovery, becoming whole, and developing their potentialities. They require each person's acknowledgment and appreciation of their differences.

6. AVOIDANCE RELATIONSHIPS. This pattern may involve people who protect themselves against any deep intimacy with others or any full contact with their own deeper feelings. Or it may involve people just coming out of a relationship who are afraid of still more of the painful feelings of loss, mourning and failure that often accompany splitting up. Or both.

7. TRANSITIONAL RELATIONSHIPS. In these, the relationship is a cross between the old and the new, between patterns that drove you crazy and others that you were changing. This lets us handle the old issues and conflicts in new ways without the gut-grinding of the old relationship. At the same time, we can try new ways of being and relating.

Can you identify the relationship that best describes your present situation? After reading this, has understanding provided the clarity you need to recognize who triggers adversity in your life. It is only after you identify the relationship, receive the understanding that you can make the proper adjustments concerning adversity. Just as situations can bring stress and tension, people can as well. Sadly, some have the best of intentions, while others seek people, such as yourself, to plant the seed of adversity in. These individuals gain great joy in stalling and ultimately stopping your process of being **"Groomed for Greatness."** Adversity becomes the tool of choice because it can be applied in layers.

The layers consist of guilt, manipulation, oppression, domination, and spirals into depression. But, because you are being **"Groomed for Greatness"** here is an excellent example of how to apply to your life as an antidote for your adversity, it is the story of the pearl.

The story of the pearl cannot be told without the piercing pain brought by the invasion of an intruders. It begins with an oyster. An oyster is defined by Merriam-Webster as a shellfish, and or any of various marine bivalve mollusks (family Ostreidae) that have a rough irregular shell closed by a single adductor muscle and include commercially important shellfish. The oyster's shell serves as external barrier of protection. It shields and defends against all threats. It is rugged and rough. It is not attractive by any means. The shell is not competing for any contest of beauty, but determine to avoid the invasion of intruders that could cause damage. It understands its role and plays it well.

TAKE THE CHALLENGE

You and I both have shells. We have created a defensive exterior shell to protect what we value as our most prized possessions. The question posed is "What other shell facades have you created to offer pseudo protection or security?" Many have made their families, lovers, friends, careers, finances, status/reputation, and influence the shells in their lives.

The problem that this presents is even with a shell, thick and rugged, adversity is inevitable. The reality of the oyster is that, despite having a shell, from time to time, some sand or small foreign particle, will breakthrough your defense system. In life even the strongest individuals find themselves weak. We attempt to locate those large things that create havoc in our lives, but honestly it the small foreign particles that we should be aware of. The oyster, after invasion has taken place, immediately deduce that a plan of action. It already has prepared itself with a strategy when invasion happens. Economics Nobel Prize laureate Prof. Israel Aumann stated: "In order to achieve peace we must first and foremost be prepared for war. We have to change this state of mind at the core."

You cannot wait until invasion to devise and develop stratagems. Prepare now and concentrate on the blueprints for your own survival, because invasion is inevitable. We can learn from the story of the oyster that when faced with intruders its response is detailed. When a pearl oyster is injured, or when it is attacked by a parasite, it will form a 'pearl sac' to contain the wound. Into this wound, the oyster secretes two proteins called conchin and perlucin. These proteins together form a matrix called conchiolin, which contains many porous spaces, somewhat like a sponge.

Into these spaces, the oyster secretes aragonite crystals. These are crystals made of calcium carbonate in the shape of tiny hexagonal plates (platelets).

Together, conchiolin and aragonite make up mother-of-pearl. When the mother-of-pearl has formed several layers around the original object, it becomes a mature pearl.

What is your response to intruders of adversity? Do you posse a "nacre" that it is secreted? Do not allow adverse objects to invade your life and infect the passions, purposes, and power you possess. As a reward and result of years of accumulation of consecutive layers of "nacre" what once:

1. **Invaded Your Privacy**
2. **Lodged in an Unwelcome Place**
3. **Refused to Move**
4. **Brought Grief and Pain**
5. **Has now become an valuable, highly sought after Pearl**

The story of the oyster fascinate and inspires me that what happens in you does not determine what will happen to you. We, like the oyster, can observe and operate with the adversity that has invaded us. We are not required to suffer in silence, but with the proper plan of action, sound stratagems, overcome the adversity that plagued us.

For many it is not an overnight experience, it could certainly take years of concentrated and calculated efforts to eliminate adversity. You and I while being **"Groomed for Greatness"** keep applying our diligence to our dilemmas, with an eye yet remaining on hope that things will get better. Sometimes the only voice of encouragement you will hear is your own, but continue to remind yourself that struggle is the badge of honor to be worn, not a burial to be placed in. Envision adversity as a cancer that is spreading across your dreams, hopes, and desires. But when attacked appropriately can work for your greater good if you remain focused on extracting the disease rather than treating the symptoms. If your support system no longer offers what you need for survival, then change your people in your system. Also, after evaluation, you could possibly need to abandon the system and solicit a new, fresh, and vibrant one that meets, speaks, and inspires you to survive.

Business Insider produced an article: 23 Incredibly Successful People Who Failed At First by Richard Feloni and Ashley Lutz on March 7, 2014. The list astounded me because each of the 23 Incredibly Successful People on the list all shared a similar thread: they suffered adversity and failed.

- ✓ **Thomas Edison's** teachers told him he was "too stupid to learn anything."

    Edison went on to hold more than 1,000 patents and invented some world-changing devices, like the phonograph, practical electrical lamp, and a movie camera.

- ✓ **Oprah Winfrey** was fired from her first television job as an anchor in Baltimore, where she said she faced sexism and harassment.

    But Winfrey rebounded and became the undisputed queen of television talk shows before amassing a media empire. Today she is worth an estimated $2.9 billion, according to Forbes.

- ✓ **Walt Disney** was fired by a newspaper editor because he "lacked imagination and had no good ideas." Several more of his businesses failed before the premiere of his movie "Snow White." Today, most childhoods wouldn't be the same without his ideas.

- ✓ **Steven Spielberg** was rejected by the University Of Southern California School Of Cinematic Arts multiple times. He went on to create the first summer blockbuster with "Jaws" in 1975, and has won three Academy Awards.

- ✓ **R.H. Macy** had a series of failed retail ventures throughout his early career. But at the age of 36, Macy launched R.H. Macy & Co., which grew to become Macy's, one of the largest department store chains in the world.

- ✓ **Vera Wang** failed to make the U.S. Olympic figure-skating team. Then she became an editor at Vogue and was passed over for the editor-in-chief position. She began designing wedding gowns at age 40 and today is one of the premier designers in the fashion industry, with a business worth over $1 billion.

- ✓ **When Sidney Poitier** first auditioned for the American Negro Theatre, he flubbed his lines and spoke in a heavy Caribbean accent, which made the director angrily tell him to stop wasting his time. Poitier worked on his craft and eventually became a hugely successful Hollywood star. He won an Academy Award for Best Actor and helped break down the color barrier in the American film industry.

Perchance the success you are so desperately trying to achieve is already within you. It is just buried under layers of adversity. Many before you, and many more after you, have tasted failure too. When the fear of failing is exposed, then the confidence to achieve is birth. Failure is possibly an indicator that success lives in you. If you settle to live with your present set of adversities, then get ready to make room for a lifetime of regret. To settle means that I am aborting the process of being "Groomed for Greatness." Remove the layers, the reward is there. Note that the list of successful people above is too exhaustive to chronicle here. Do not allow the list to conclude before you name and experience are added.

Affirmation

> "Not everyone can be famous but everyone can be great, Because greatness is determined." - Dr. Martin L. King, Jr.

Charles T. Schmidt, Jr- The University of Rhode Island (Labor Research Center) produced an article entitled "Affirming Behaviors." This excerpt best defines **Affirmation**:

An important element of the self-concept motivation theory is a concept of affirmation (also called validation or reinforcement). Individuals constantly seek to validate their self-perceptions by looking for feedback from the results of their activities (Task Feedback) and from the behavior and comments of others (Social Feedback). Affirming behavior refers to the words and deeds of others that act to reinforce an individual's self-perceptions of competencies, traits, and values. This section will discuss the ways in which the behavior of others acts to validate or invalidate one's self concept. A simple smile, nodding of the head, and exciting facial expression all serve as indicators of validation. The pre-school boy who answers correctly, to the adult who completes the assignment at work, affirmation is appreciated by everyone.

It is interesting the affects that affirmation, or the lack thereof, has on a person from the crib of childhood to rocking chair of elderly. Validation has an astounding way of shaping the confidence, while invalidation has a damaging effect on the individuals psyche. It causes one to soar with self-assurance, whereas the other is left with a tower of questions that have no answers. They both should proceed with caution, because all behavior is subject to interpretation. Self-worth will accept or reject affirmation based on personal evaluation of its value.

I have met some really beautiful people in my life. Their physical attraction was obvious to everyone. The ideal weight, shape and hair length. Sadly it was oblivious to the person. Because they lacked self-worth, no matter the level of affirmation it, was never received. They vehemently expressed that what others saw in them, was not viewed by themselves. Similarly, I am privileged to know some talented individuals. Their abilities would mesmerized the masses and they struggle with low or no self-confidence. They had "out-front" stardom, but chose the "back-ground" shadows. In the shadows of the "back-ground" it is a sense of safety. If they were to strike the wrong chord, sing the incorrect lyrics with an off note, perhaps no one would even notice.

It was reported on www.bustle.com (Bustle is for and by women who are moving forward as fast as you are- Providing Non-Stop News) that 47 percent of Young Girls are Held Back by Low Self-Esteem, And That's Not Ok. The article based the spike and rise in percentage is due to the lack of affirmation. The study cited girls between the ages of 11-14 who refused to participate in school activities where the bodies were exposed (such as swimming, physical education, etc.) because of the lack of confidence. Though the study was UK based, there is no doubt that body confidence, and the lack thereof, impacts girls and women on a severe emotional and physical level worldwide, from the UK and the US to China and Venezuela.

Marie Southhard Ospina, Contributing Writer for Bustle state; 47 percent. That's nearly HALF of young teen girls refusing to participate in all those activities that are an essential part of growing up — like playing outside, going to the beach, joining clubs at school.

Of course, the tale of the plus-size 13-year-old who was too embarrassed to wear a bikini because her peers would make fun of her is not a surprising one. But it seems the problem has extended beyond what it used to be. Where before, self-esteem issues seemed to plague the outcasts — the bullied — they now plague half of all girls.

Girls who are probably an average weight. Girls who are probably beautiful. Girls who have nothing wrong with them. Justin Healey, author of Body Image and Self Esteem, found that "concern about how their body looks is now the biggest worry for the nation's 11 to 24-year-olds" where as in 2006, body image ranked third after family conflicts and alcohol/drug related worries. The DSEP study also reveals that 49 percent of girls in this age bracket need words of encouragement from their mothers to branch out and join clubs. And 23 percent are too afraid to put their hand up in class. As Yahoo writer Sophie Tighe pointed out, "It doesn't bode well for the future of female leaders and businesswomen." She really nailed it on the head. If young women are showing serious signs of body anxiety from age 11, what hope is there that they will become confident and empowered women?

As always, one wonders how much the media plays into the situation, or how much parenting has to do with it. How much can we blame this problem on the images of emaciated teeny-bopper celebrities that pervade the major networks? WebMD's Elizabeth Heubeck says "researchers found that TV programs focused on appearance are swaying the self-esteem of girls as young as five." How much can we blame the parent who didn't tell her kid she was pretty enough? According to the Office on Women's Health, it's been proven that complimenting your kid on his/her "efforts, talents, accomplishments and personal values" goes way further in the aid of body confidence than critiquing the child's aesthetics.

Types of affirming behavior

Here is a list of kinds of behavior that individuals often view as affirming in terms of their acceptance in the group, the value of their competencies, their contribution to the group, and their status within the group. They range from simple signals of acceptance and liking to important signals of strong attachment.

- Facial expressions and body language indicating that somebody is glad to see you.
- Inclusion of you in events and activities, such as asking you to lunch/inviting parties.
- Following your advice.
- Positive feedback and recognition of skills and worth
- Sharing important information with you or other indications of trust.

✓ **Trusting behavior is one of the most validating types of behavior.**
- Choosing to spend time with you when there are other motivating options.
- Showing concern for your well-being.
- Taking time to listen to your problems and showing empathy.
- Recognizing significant achievements. Remembering important things about you.

The list could be endless depending on the individual's needs for Affirmation.

Basic Principle

A basic principle in writing is that one should never edit or proof their own work. The affirmation of someone you trust is invaluable. It is difficult for the same set of eyes that produced it to find errors to critique and criticize. You are passionate about it, or you should be. The exhausting hours and time devoted to the project speaks volumes of your dedication. We give concessions for what we adore. The boundaries are extended, and we overlook the obvious, and miss the major details. The spell check does ask your permission to flag your errors. If your system is set to auto-correct, it will automatically replace it for you. Affirmation correctively critiques. Just as auto-correct, it provides an assurance that your greatest intentions are articulated correctly. The problem with "self-proofing" is that our intentions are not always in step with our presentation. Affirmation serves as the "spell check" to flag our errors, before production, then corrections are made, and embarrassment is eliminated. Remember, even greatness requires editing. No one arrives at the station of greatness, parks, and remains there. There are constant updates, and reminders that are needful to maintain this status. Just as greatness just does not happen, remaining great requires a continual commitment to the details. I dare to say the thing that distinguishes those who are good from those who are great is attention to details. Affirmation can serve as the spirit within great people for perfection. The project could easily pass the inspection of others, but perfectionist eye details. They want to ensure that no stone has been left unturned, and every principle protected.

This spirit of affirmation would literally drive one crazy and irritate others, but not you. It is in the details that determine the success or failure you will have. The little thing that others overlook that seem so insignificant. It's worth going the extra mile and that's being "Groomed for Greatness."

Builders Create Blinders

Here is another principle: "What is created and transferred, are shared thoughts in their purest form." It is only the mind that cultivates the thoughts that truly understands its ultimate intentions. Thus builders create blinders. These blinders allow the one building to see into it only what they desire. From their perception the destination is clear although not one step has been made on the journey. Blinders are best used when training horses to be great. Blinders, or blinkers and winkers, as they are otherwise known, are a part of the tatic used on many horses. Blinders are small squares of firm leather that attach to the bridle at the side of the horse's head. They keep the horse's eyes focused on what is ahead, rather than what is at the side or behind. Affirmation serves those being "Groomed for Greatness" in the same capacity. It assist to remove the distractions from what travels from our past to paralyze us. Affirmation in the form of blinders, blinkers, and winkers trains the individual not to lose focus. It does not privilege one to see what others are doing and subsequently measure themselves by others accomplishments. Use affirmation to stay focus on what is ahead.

Critique Correctly

Who critiques you is far greater than what they are critiquing. The price of validation from the wrong person can be costly. Affirmation spends the treasured time to locate someone in whom trust is found as their lone motivator. The process of critiquing is sensitive and you will appreciate someone who can speak truth in love. The harshness of abrasive attitudes can completely destroy the creativity of being "Groomed for Greatness." Love will ease the sting of truth. Affirmation will assist in securing someone whose motives are to make you better. They should serve as skilled surgeon for you and not a butcher. Both require trained persons. Both involve cutting, it's a difference of instruments that differentiate them one from another. The butcher is highly skilled and qualified. The butcher no doubt takes their profession very seriously. The butcher understands the importance to details. The only issue is that the product butcher is working with has reached its destination. The surgeon is yet working with something that has life and potential. The surgeon understands that each incision is precise and delicate. Their professionalism is corroborated in their ability to close incisions that create with stitches that eventually heal.

So, affirmation interviews who has the potential to kill or heal you. Then and only then, will it provide a platform to speak into your life. It is rendered voiceless until validated. All affirmations are needed and some are not needful.

Who and what you allow to speak you're your life will determine your destiny (predetermined course of events often held to be an irresistible power of agency) and destination (a place to which one is journeying or to which something is sent). Critiquing correctly ensures life and truth has provided necessary cuts.

It warrants wounds that over time will close completely. It holds your hand while walking you down the corridor of maturity.

When Affirmation Goes Wrong

The balance of the scales of success is not only to reveal what is needful, but what is not as well. There numerous factors that can affirm and affect you negatively. You see, you have two basic parts to your mind, your conscious, and you're subconscious. Which mind do you think has more effect over your day-to-day actions? Affirmation from others is fickle and fleeting.

If you answered "subconscious," you're correct. It's pretty much universally agreed that the subconscious mind is the main driver of human behavior. While we may think that we rationalize and make our decisions from our logical, conscious mind, what typically happens is we first make a decision from our subconscious mind, and then find conscious reasons to support it.

In any case, the subconscious is the real driver. These negative affirming factors live here. They speak to our subconscious vociferously. It is the voice you hear that reprimands you for a mistake you made. It is the overwhelming sense of guilt felt from not doing something you were prompted to. These negative affirming factors use manipulation as a vehicle to drive you to great distances of disappointment. It employs domination as well to coerce you into taking the ride of resentment where you abort what you are passionate about. The entire journey is filled with the battle of mixed emotions.

Punctured Potential

If you are used to hearing negative comments from others and in particular if you suffer from verbal abuse, then you may be at risk of becoming a victim even if that abuse stops. What sometimes happens is that some people get so used to verbal abuse and insults they actually come to expect them and this is why some people seem to continually get caught up in abusive relationships and accept it. You do not deserve to put up with this if this is something in your life. No-one should accept abuse as normal.

Low Self esteem

Messages that you get can really affect you negatively. Imagine someone who is subjected to negative comments all day long at work. Because of the money people in jobs like this sometimes just put up with this but the result is low self-esteem. Likewise, what your partner says to you or what parents or friends say may stick in your mind and damage your self-esteem if you let it.

One of the worst things for your self-esteem is self-talk. This is what you say to yourself. We are often our worst judge. If you fail in some way the things you say to yourself will reflect in how you feel about yourself. If you have to listen to negative messages from others then you need to be extra supportive to you. Positive self-talk will encourage you and make you strong enough to withstand the negativity outside of you and even to ignore it.

Complicate Your Creativity

The biggest problem if you want to start thinking positively and end your destructive negativity, is that those kind of thoughts have probably become habit by now. As we all now breaking a habit is not easy.

Before you even try to break a habit you better be 100% sure you want to do this. It will require some hard work. What is the secret to breaking a habit? Create a new one in its place.

Creating the habit of thinking positively needs a change in your attitude first. It is not difficult to write out some helpful positive affirmations and then repeat them often to yourself but nothing will happen unless you also change your attitude.

To help you with this here are areas to concentrate on:

- Understand and convince yourself that you are born to be a winner. Losing is what happens when you stop yourself from succeeding.
- Don't forget that you should enjoy the journey towards achieving your goal. If you keep thinking about the end result as a means to happiness you will never be happy.
- Many of your negative beliefs may be wrong. How many of the limits you place on yourself are real? How many come from negative comments you got as you grew up? Question the truth of these beliefs. Create new more positive ones that will help you.
- Try to treat yourself better. Do you know that most people treat themselves very badly? If you think you should treat others with kindness then why do you not do the same for you?

Dependent on Dysfunction

One of the greatest obstacles to your success is not fear of failure, as most people think but fear of success. You may have spent such a long time seeing yourself as a failure, that if you begin to work towards positive change, you may face the thought that success could also be scary. You see anything new can be seen as either positive or negative. New challenges and opportunities for one person may be seen as risky and dangerous to another. This is becoming dependent on your dysfunction. You rely more on the negative than the positive. The effects of this dysfunction has rendered you helpless and hopeless. What kind of person do you want to be? Do you want to change things even if it means taking a small risk where the rewards are huge, or will you continue to be a fearful person, who would rather remain unhappy than take a chance to change things?

Fear of success results in self-sabotage. Put simply, you will do things to prevent being successful. You may not even know you are doing this. Examine what you want and determine how you will get it. You can stop you're dependence on dysfunction. The desire to do so must come from within you. The desire will not fully develop if it for someone else. You must want this for yourself. Do not place lofty or unattainable goals as you're focus. This is the proverbial cartoon of the carrot dangling over the head of the runner. They are simply chasing with every fiber of endurance something that will never be obtained.

What steps will you take? What will success change in your life? See it in your mind and feel it? Make sure you are totally ready to be successful and that you really want that.

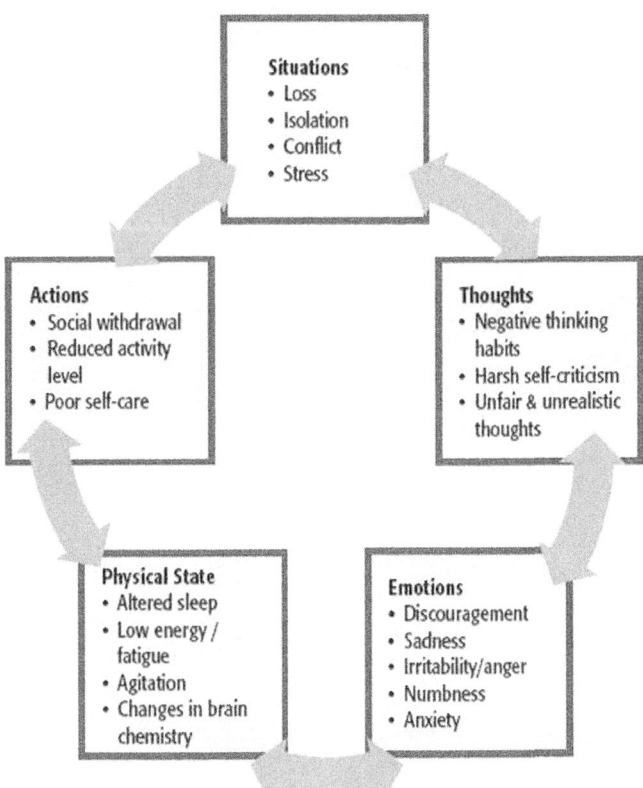

ACHIEVEMENT

"You were put on this earth to achieve your greatest self, to live out purpose, and to do it fearlessly." – Steve Maraboli

July 25, 2012- Nike launched "Find Your Greatness" Campaign. It is not just the championship athlete or record breaker that aspires to push their limits. It is also the everyday athlete who strives to excel on their own terms, to set and realize personal goals and achieve their own defining moment of greatness. That's the insight behind Nike's "Find Your Greatness" campaign, a powerful message to inspire anyone who wants to achieve their own moment of greatness in sport, launched just as the world focuses on the best of the best.

"The idea behind 'Find Your Greatness' is simply to inspire and energize everyday athletes everywhere to celebrate their achievements, participate and enjoy the thrill of achieving in sport at their own level," said Greg Hoffman, Nike VP of Brand Design & Communications. In effect, greatness has no fixed address but is a place where every athlete can achieve their own personal success and shape their own definition.

While being "Groomed for Greatness" this chapter is significant to your success. I challenge you to "Find Your Greatness" by striving to excel on your own terms, set and realize personal goals and achieve your own defining moments of greatness. This challenge is to complete unfinished projects and assignments. To go back and pick up the pieces of your purpose that were dropped due to unforeseen hindrances and or deliberate obstacles placed in your path. Are you ready for the challenge? The rewards are life changing achievements that defines your greatness.

To achieve greatness in your life there are some "bedrocks" and foundational truths that you must develop and incorporate daily. These set of "low points" and tenets, principles, or axioms will serve as the landmarks on the journey to Achievement while being "Groomed for Greatness." They will serve as the "secrets to your success" that fuel you when you are running low and near empty. You can employ them as motivators when affirmation seems lacking and longing. It is best to set them before the journey begins to enact a sense of security when everything in life is telling you're lost or the destination is not obtainable. The bedrocks/ foundational truths will act as reminders that you have not arrived yet, but celebrate how far you have travelled. Are you ready to begin? Let's "Find Your Greatness" and reside and retire there.

<u>Bedrock/Foundational Truth #1-</u>

"Achieving Greatness is a Journey, not a Destination"

When you arrive at achievement, you will have discovered that greatness is a journey travelled, not a destination reached. I continued to make the mistake of announcing anticipated deadlines and deliveries of this very book. The pressure of not completing this task became prodigious. I began placing unachievable goals upon myself, writing in sporadic spurts and reading and researching at very odd times. My regiment and schedule was toxic and taxing. For me writing had lost its sense of luster, joy, and ultimate purpose. I was now trying to reach a destination, rather than enjoying the journey it was taking me on. My preoccupation with meeting the expectation of others, caused me to omit the very reason why I have always enjoyed writing. Real honest writers (or anyone who produces something from their passion) will admit that underlying motivating factor is to encourage, inspire, educate, and assist others.

People of passion almost never produce what is within them for the love of money, things, or approval of others. It was only then that I slammed the brakes on my "unachievable goals" and reminded myself that my destination had not changed, but enjoying the journey did. Those sporadic spurts changed into scheduled times for meditation and commitment to the process. I had to stop and embrace the journey I was on. Granting myself permission again to appreciate what was to encourage others. To sample the unfinished product, and take delight in it.

Most of my early life experiences were shared with my great-grandmother, Florence Hicks. She lived to reach the milestone age of 105. I vividly remember spending countless summers at her home in Eutaw, Alabama. She was an amazing cook. I developed the principle of 'sampling the unfinished product' from her. Each morning before the sun rose, she was up and prepping for the tasks of that day. Her routine was extraordinary to say the least. In the bed nightly by 7pm, but up every morning by 4:30am. While everyone else in the house was snuggled in their beds, draped with custom quilts she and her mother made by hand, Mrs. Hicks was up cooking breakfast. She would have pots and pans on the stove, while baking biscuits in the oven, moving in synchronization like a conductor in front of grand orchestra. Every now and then, she would uncover a pot or pan and insert a spoon and carefully blow to cool and then taste. Her intentions were not to eat the food, but just sample it. She would either emphatically nod in approval, or frown in dejection. The product was not far from completion, but she knew that sampling the unfinished products would safeguard embarrassment later. If she was not satisfied, immediate adjustments were made. That valuable lesson has remained with me to this day. I apply it to cooking and or projects I am producing. This principle has saved me from embarrassment and supplied the confidence when the task is complete. Sampling the unfinished product allows the first and foremost important critique to come from me. It permits me the privilege to omit the criticism of others who can be overbearing and insensitive.

You can make the necessary adjustments in private before public opinions are ever created. These adjustments are little reminders to yourself that no one operates in perfection. Even the best at craft have to make adjustments along the way. On this journey, your destination is not changing, but the scenery will. I must admit that not only the scenery will have modifications, but people who occupy the seats on your journey are subject to change as well.

I gave a lecture on the significance of **"Learning from a Layover"** to enthusiastic and energetic crowd. My dissertation was developed on the main theme, that when traveling by plane, your connections are inevitable. The people who began the first segment (departure) of the trip with you, will not necessarily travel with you to the end (destination). You cannot become so connected with others that you miss your connection. Although it is true, you all boarded the same aircraft, from the same gate, in the same city, your destinations could all be different. The connection or layover, is intentional to separate you from those who are no longer traveling in your direction, but also to connect you "new" people who are. On this journey do not confuse your travel plan with your travel partners. Enjoy the journey that life is taking you on presently. One of particular reasons I have mandated enjoying the journey, because life in itself is guaranteed to have longevity.

When you relax and enjoy the journey, appreciation for others will serve as landmark for Achievement. So many people listed being unappreciated as key factor in divorce and a seedbed for unhappiness. The destination is fixed, but the journey should be enjoyed.

Bedrock/Foundational Truth #2-
"To Achieve Greatness, Quitting is Not an Option"

There are 3 types of people in the world one quote stated;

1. **Those Who Make Things Happen**
2. **Those Who Watch Things Happen**
3. **Those Who Ask "What" Happen**

Greatness is developed based on how you define the aforementioned. How do you see yourself? Which one of the statements above defines you? People of greatness vacillate from #1 and #2, very rarely are they #3. Because most people who have determined that greatness is destined for them, have an insatiable attitude not to quit or give up. The motto the live by is, "I would rather give out before giving up." They understand that the trait of quitting cannot live in the DNA of people of greatness.

I need to add clarity that I am in wise saying people of greatness do not fail or fall, they just do not remain there. The understanding is that there is no shame in falling or failing, because "greatness" is not often recognized or revered. While being "Groomed for Greatness" it is vital that negotiate within yourself that "Quitting is Not an Option" for you. Life will surely deliver some heartfelt blows from time to time, but champions never win the title without taking some punches. Muhammad Ali is considered one of the greatest athletes in boxing history, winning both the coveted Golden Gloves title and an Olympic gold medal, among several other honors.

Bedrock/Foundational Truth #3-
"Achieving Greatness, You Must Have a Firm Foundation"

Ali showed at an early age that he wasn't afraid of any bout—inside or outside of the ring. Growing up in the segregated South, Ali experienced racial prejudice and discrimination firsthand, which likely contributed to his early passion for boxing. At the age of 12, Ali discovered his talent for boxing through an odd twist of fate. His bike was stolen, and Ali told a police officer, Joe Martin, that he wanted to beat up the thief. "Well, you better learn how to fight before you start challenging people," Martin reportedly told him at the time. In addition to being a police officer, Martin also trained young boxers at a local gym.

Ali started working with Martin to learn how to box, and soon began his boxing career. In his first amateur bout in 1954, he won the fight by split decision. Ali went on to win the 1956 Golden Gloves tournament for novices in the light heavyweight class. Three years later, he won the National Golden Gloves Tournament of Champions, as well as the Amateur Athletic Union's national title for the light-heavyweight division. In 1960, Ali won a spot on the U.S. Olympic boxing team. He traveled to Rome, Italy, to compete. At 6 feet 3 inches tall, Ali was an imposing figure in the ring. He was known for his footwork, and for possessing a powerful jab. After winning his first three bouts, Ali then defeated Zbigniew Pietrzkowski from Poland to win the gold medal.

After his Olympic victory, Ali was heralded as an American hero. He soon turned professional with the backing of the Louisville Sponsoring Group. During the 1960s Ali seemed unstoppable, winning all of his bouts with majority of them being by knockouts. He took out British heavyweight champion Henry Cooper in 1963 and then knocked out Sonny Liston in 1964 to become the heavyweight champion of the world.

Often referring to himself as "the greatest," Ali was not afraid to sing his own praises. He was known for boasting about his skills before a fight and for his colorful descriptions and phrases. In one of his more famously quoted descriptions, Ali told reporters that he could "float like a butterfly, sting like a bee" in the boxing ring.

In the process of researching some of his famous quotes, I discovered an entire site dedicated to Ali's sayings. People of greatness need to be talkative. To others as well as to themselves. You must dare call yourself what others will not. Ali called himself the greatest, when there were others who could box better, had more experience, and just as gifted. The only difference is that Ali believed the words he told everyone about himself. The label of arrogance was placed on him. Many indicated that he was supercilious and pompous. But, it never made Ali quit, because I believe he was talking more to himself than others. He was a master at defeating his opponents with his mouth, before ever laying a fist on them.

Bedrock/Foundational Truth #4-

"Achieving Greatness, Will Require What Others Are Not Willing To Give"

In article- Muhammad Ali: "The Greatest"- by Joyce Carol Oates First published in ESPN Sports Century, New York: Hyperion, 1999. Reprinted in Uncensored: Views & Reviews stated:

> "No other athlete has received quite the press—accusing and adulatory, condemning and praising, seething with hatred and brimming with love—that Ali has had. From the first, as the young Cassius Clay, he seems to have determined that he would not be a passive participant in his image-making, like most athletes, but would define the terms of his public reputation.

As sport is both a mirror of human aggression and a highly controlled, "playful" acting-out of that aggression, so the public athlete is a play-figure, at his most conscious and controlled an actor in a theatrical event. Clay/Ali brought to the deadly-serious sport of boxing an unexpected ecstatic joy that had nothing to do with, and may in fact have been contrary to, his political/religious mission. His temperament seems to have been fundamentally childlike; playing the trickster came naturally to him, "My corn, the gimmicks, the acting I do—it'll take a whole lot for another fighter to ever be as popular as Muhammad Ali," he remarked in an interview in 1975. "The acting begins when I'm working. Before a fight, I'll try to have something funny to say every day and I'll talk ten miles a minute . . . I started fighting in 1954, when I was just twelve, so it's been a long time for me now. But there's always a new fight to look forward to, a new publicity stunt, a new reason to fight."

Quitting is Not an Option for people of greatness. The ability to talk to the very nemesis that is deterring you, and defeat it before it can defeat you speaks to greatness. Quitting is easy. Giving up is status quo for others, but not you. If you took a thorough inventory of the successes in your life, it would amaze you that beside every great feat, is a potential defeat. The determination to win was greater than succumbing to quitting. Winners display a "swagger" an attitude of self-confidence that hinges on being pompous and threatens superciliousness. They understand that they cannot control the outcome of the game. The only thing they could do is leave all they have on the floor. "I hated every minute of training, but I said, "Don't quit. Suffer now and live the rest of your life as a champion."- I am the greatest, I said that even before I knew I was. -Muhammad Ali

Bedrock/Foundational Truth #5-
"To Achieve Greatness, Glance at the Gauges"

Even champions face fatigue and need refueling to achieve their goals. It is not different for you. This bedrock/foundational truth is fundamental because you can posse great skills, but with low to no stamina, you will not achieve greatness.

People can have the outstanding drive and potential, but when your proverbial "tank" is empty, the goals set are insurmountable.

Glance at your gauges to determine on this journey where you are and how far you can continue. There is a profound difference in glancing and staring? Glancing entails making sudden quick contact with an intentional mark, to touch on a subject or refer to it briefly and indirectly.

They importance here is to employ brevity. Staring on the other hand, implies to look fixedly often with wide-open eyes, to show oneself conspicuously, securely placed on fastened, to become stationary. While being "Groomed for Greatness" it is essential to major in glancing at the gauges and to minor in staring at them. This will prevent what every person of greatness battles, "Burn Out." It is when that proverbial "tank" has been exhausted and no energy, excitement, nor enthusiasm is left. The feeling is disheartening because the body is working against itself. Your mind is either telling your body to keep up when it cannot, or your body is yelling at your mind to do the same. The fatigue factor sets in and "burn-out" is inevitable and a domino effect in progress. It seems as if one thing after, the succession of collapse is apparent.

Many years ago I was fortunate to work for some major airlines. One of the many perks of being employed by these companies was the outstanding travel benefits. This was based on the availability of flights and required a level of skill, research, and constant updating in some cases.

We are instructed to check all flight options and choose several paths to your destination. Because we worked for the airline, it did not guarantee us a seat, if a paying customer desired to travel.

Things could seem so promising until the very last moment (literal minutes) prior to departure that a potential empty seat could become occupied. Glancing at the gauges became an art form and science. The principle is that 5 minutes before the scheduled departure time all unclaimed seats are released. You check your gauges to see how many people have booked the flight. Then the number people who had other plans, and decided to standby for that same particular flight. You check your gauges to determine the number of open seats against the number of standbys.

Lastly, there is a "priority list" this is regulated by the individual's seniority. This list governs the selection progress. I had to remember that the priority list was not prejudice to me, nor was it personal. The names listed where given priority for specific reasons. Individuals were instructed to keep watching the list on monitors. This was important because once your name is called you must respond immediately. If there is no response when a name is called, the next person receives their priority.

All of this happens within a 3-5 minute window. I have stood seconds ready to board an aircraft only to be pulled because a "runner" reached the gate prior to departure.

Now, there are some major "Groomed for Greatness" principles I outlined for you.

1. **Glancing at the Gauges** does not guarantee everything will work as planned. It only serves to keep you updated on everything happening.
2. **Glancing at the Gauges** will not override the process. Despite disappointment, knowing the facts will protect you from failure.
3. **Glancing at the Gauges** cannot change the principles. It ensures that you make a decision you have the all the proper data to do so.

4. **Glancing at the Gauges** do not permit you to become comfortable in critical moments, but it will provide confidence that you have done all you can.

You develop a "toughness" that if the process does not work in my favor, then I obeyed the rules, and I have other options. It is the ingredient of ingenuity that people of greatness possess, that problematic situations authorize them to locate within themselves. A "stick-to-it-ness" that becomes the fuel to new and vibrant ideas that seemingly where not present.

It provides answers to the staring question of **"What Next"** that failure will continue to whisper until it drains you. This ingredient of ingenuity serves to add flavor to a bland situation. It gives the situation a touch that was obviously missing from the beginning. You did not add it before, because it had not revealed that it was needed.

Glancing at the Gauges:

Burn-out occurs when we give out more than we take in. We go from giving out to giving up. Cars that aren't refueled will run out of gas. Wells that are not replenished will run dry. Batteries that are not recharged will have no power. We are not any different. A person being "Groomed for Greatness" that is not refueled, replenished, and recharged will burn out. See chart provided below.

Lateness Behavior	Pattern	Frequency	Duration
Increasing Chronic	Nonrandom	Increasing	Increasing
Stable Periodic	Nonrandom	Stable	Stable
Unavoidable	Random	Immeasurable	Immeasurable

DEVELOPING YOUR PERSISTENCE: Harold Sherman, author of *How to Turn Failure into Success,* has written a code of persistence. While being "Groomed for Greatness" I encourage you to memorize these principles tenaciously.

1. I will never give up so long as I know I am right.
2. I believe that all things will work out if I hang on.

3. I will be courageous & undismayed in the face of poor odds.

4. I will not permit anyone to intimidate/ deter me from my goals.

5. I will fight to overcome all physical handicaps & setbacks.

6. I will try again & again & yet again to accomplish my desires.

7. I will take new faith & resolution from the knowledge that all successful men & women have had to fight defeat & adversity.

8. I will never surrender to discouragement or despair no matter what seeming obstacles may confront me.

ACCOMPLISHMENT

"To be yourself in a world that is constantly trying to make you something else is the greatest accomplishment."- Ralph Waldo Emerson

Achievement and **Accomplishment** are two-stem words seemingly used interchangeably to mean the same with slight shade of difference. **Achievement** is most commonly associated with a letter grade, percentile, standardized mean, or other metric. A relentless pursuit of an A grade often obscures, if not obstructs, the learning process. The grade as instructional product - rather than learning as educational process - distorts achievement. Positive psychology suggests that there is a distinction between achievement that is focused on quantitative scores and accomplishment that is focused on qualitative results.

Achievement typically measures an externally imposed standard.

Accomplishment typically describes an internally motivated goal.

Accomplishment is the inventory of what children have done well in the past and what they aspire to do well in the future for personal satisfaction and lasting fulfillment.

Accomplishment is the pursuit and practice of academic, social, emotional intentions and excellence at home, at work, at school, and at play, meeting personal goals, and deriving satisfaction from the process.

An accomplished child or youth is elected leader in the friendship club, plays the piano because he loves music, and reads a book because he is curious about a subject. He studies for a test because he wants to do well, writes a letter because he misses his aunt, draws a picture because it calms him, acts brave because others are counting on him, and teaches tolerance because he empathizes with the sting of unfair treatment.

An accomplished child or youth sorts out emotions when confused, engages strength when discouraged, makes friends when lonely, summons courage when called to it, contributes in meaningful ways when uncertain, and enjoys authentic accomplishment as the fruit of their labor.

Students learn to leverage their emotional skills to accomplish their personal and academic goals. The goal of positive psychology is to systematically teach children about their emotionality, their strengths, the requirements of friendships, the meaning of life, and to take pride in their efforts and accomplishments.

The accomplishment that begets success requires deferred gratification, self-efficacy, and tenacity that empower determination and motivation despite adversity. The measure of the positive psychology teaching taxonomy of success is the degree to which children can establish personal goals, direct effort toward those goals, and accomplish them or edit them with equanimity.

If children and adolescent truly know their emotions, can identify their strengths, can build grit, connect with others, can find meaning no matter the tasks, and can become accomplished classroom citizens, they will achieve more academically. Achievement is a by-product of accomplishment. The accomplished student knows an 'A' is more than three sticks.

There is an "Art to Accomplishment." No one stumbles into success. It is calculated, considered, and deliberate. There are strategic steps that one is required to make in order to obtain Accomplishment. When the steps are skipped then the longevity of Accomplishment is in jeopardy. This methodical and systematic process only imbues the fragrance of favor that is a chief ingredient to Accomplishment. The steps serve as a recipe that when properly mixed and carefully stirred, that final product of Accomplishment is delivered.

Would you like to know the recipe? Well, here it is.

"The Art to Accomplishment"

1 full cup of- Clear Concise Goals

½ ounce of- Describing It

½ ounce of- Defining It

½ ounce of- Developing It

1 full cup of- Motivation

½ pound of- Making your Move

½ pound of- Motivational Markers

½ pound of- Meaningful Management

1 full cup of- Seriousness

½ gallon of- Creating Momentum

½ gallon of- Chasing Momentum

½ gallon of- Completing Momentum

Ready, let's go!

Clear & Concise

1. Be Clear

When writing or speaking to someone, be clear about your goal or message. What is your purpose in communicating with this person? If you're not sure, then your audience won't be sure either. To be clear, try to minimize the number of ideas in each sentence. Make sure that it's easy for your reader to understand your meaning. People shouldn't have to "read between the lines" and make assumptions on their own to understand what you're trying to say.

Here is a Bad Example:

Hi John,

I wanted to write you a quick note about Daniel, who's working in your department. He's a great asset, and I'd like to talk to you more about him when you have time.

Best,

Skip

What is this email about? Well, we're not sure. First, if there are multiple Daniels in John's department, John won't know who Skip is talking about. Next, what is Daniel doing, specifically, that's so great? We don't know that either.

It's so vague that John will definitely have to write back for more information. Last, what is the purpose of this email? Does Skip simply want to have an idle chat about Daniel, or is there some more specific goal here? There's no sense of purpose to this message, so it's a bit confusing.

Now, here is a Good Example:

Hi John,

I wanted to write you a quick note about Daniel Kedar, who's working in your department. In recent weeks, he's helped the IT department through several pressing deadlines on his own time.

We've got a tough upgrade project due to run over the next three months, and his knowledge and skills would prove invaluable. Could we please have his help with this work? I'd appreciate speaking with you about this. When is it best to call you to discuss this further?

Best wishes,

Skip

This second message is much clearer, because the reader has the information he needs to take action. As you strive for Accomplishment, "Be Clear" and articulate your message without an ounce of doubt. This step, as small as it may seem, will save you valuable time and energy in the process. You do not want to arrive at "Accomplishment" only to discover that your goals did not provide enough clarity. Trust me, it is worth every single sacrifice to cover the bases. Remember, your ascension from Assessments to Accomplishments is only as solid as the clarity it rest upon. There is an amazing feeling that accompanies "Accomplishment" and it cannot be impersonated. You cannot substitute it, nor should desire to. To "Be Clear" is defined as easily heard, easily seen through, free from doubt, and free from obscurity or ambiguity.

2. Be Concise

When you're concise in your goal setting for Accomplishment, you stick to the point and keep it brief. You do not want to read six sidebars or digressions when you could communicate your goals in three. In describing the concept of being "Concise" answer the following questions:

- Are there any obstacles or "fillers" that you can delete?
- Are there any unnecessary goals set for Accomplishment?
- Have you repeated the goal several times, just in different ways?
- Are you sabotaging your own Accomplishment?

In the process of being "Groomed for Greatness" you can often eliminate obvious obstacles to Accomplishment. A mentor once told me, "There is a major difference in dreaming and hallucinating. The problem is being concise to remove them from the same space." Being "Concise" is an excellent accompaniment to clarity in pursuit of Accomplishment. While being clear- is defined as easily heard, easily seen through, free from doubt, and free from obscurity or ambiguity, it is the ability to become concise that adds to Accomplishment. Concise is using few words: not including extra or unnecessary information. To be aphoristic, apothegmatic, brief, compact, compendious elliptical (or elliptic), sententious, and succinct. It is the capability to express much with less. This is a key principle, because life will challenge you, from time to time, to live extravagant and elaborate. When modesty meets the margin of the day.

I exercise the K.I.S.S. rule- Keep It Super Simple. This rule has aided me in "reeling it in" over the span of my life in pursuit of Accomplishment.

Granted, extravagancy and engaging in the elaborate and opulent can seem ostentatious to others. It must be meet with a "Clear and Concise" approach to ensure Accomplishment is never mismanaged. The K.I.S.S. rule is bathe in brevity. The principle states that most systems work best if they are kept simple rather than made complicated; therefore simplicity should be a key goal in design and unnecessary complexity should be avoided. The phrase has been associated with aircraft engineer Kelly Johnson (1910–1990). The term "KISS principle" was in popular use by 1970. Variations on the phrase include "keep it short and simple", "keep it simple and straightforward" and "keep it small and simple".

Anatole France- was a French poet, journalist, and novelist who made this statement- "To accomplish great things we must dream as well as act." This is the balance needed in your quest for "Accomplishment" of anything of significance. Being "Concise" will provide you with the courage to walk the tightrope from goal perceived to goal achieved. The elimination of "collected clutter" will serve as a support to the conception of being "Concise."

Motivation

1. Making Your Move

Chinese philosopher Lao Tzu was pointed and profound when he stated- "The journey of a thousand miles begins with one step." To "Accomplish" anything in life it begins with that first step and then a series of methodical steps thereafter. Making your move is yes filled with risk, but reward is the seed inside of it. If you take an apple, cut it into two halves, you can see possibilities in the number seeds it possess. As you began to count the seeds, it is apparent that being "Groomed for Greatness" has striking similarities. You will never know until you make the move to cut it. The number seeds inside the apple reveals something to powerful. If you count the number of seeds, you can accurately assess the number of seeds were in the apple, but you cannot determine how many trees where in the seeds. This journey you have embarked upon began with making your move with one step.

You will never experience the opulent odious aroma that emerges from "Accomplishment" until you make your move. There is a scent to success. It is attractive and addictive. This step seemingly simple to make, can become the sore of sensitivity in one's life. Making your move is the defining factor that yields great dividends. It imbues a confidence and builds character, but you will not have the knowledge of it until you do it. There is a synergy that surfaces from "Making Your Move" that last a lifetime.

The pitfalls of the Deception of Perception is important when taking that first of many steps. Do not become confused because of the lack of clarity, remember- "BE CONCISE" is critical.

I was watching a football game, one of my favorite excuses for downtime, and notice this principle being illustrated. On this particular play, the quarterback attempted to throw a pass to an open teammate. He caught the pass and proceeded to run down the field for what seemed an easy touchdown. To his surprise the opposing team's players interrupted his intentions causing a fumble. When the player, on the opposing team, picked up the fumbled ball, he began to run for a touchdown. In just a split second, the tide turned and faces in the stadium told the entire story. The sidelines both erupted, one in spontaneous elation, while the other in sheer embarrassment. As the player was running the ball, interestingly, the coach and other players were running down the sideline with him.

The Deception of Perception is to become preoccupied with sideline activity. If not careful you will remove attention from the person of prominence with the ball to those whose opinion in the matter has no effect on the outcome. While both were running with enthusiasm and excitement and the fans cheering and yelling for both. The one with the ball in his hand only mattered.

The guys on the sideline were running out of option, but the player on the field was running out of obligation. Making your move began with the player deciding to pick up the ball because he was in the right position at the right time. You must seize the opportunity that is being presented to you. This could be one of those "once in a lifetime" opportunities. Take full advantage of this moment and maximize it.

Lastly, be careful in your pursuit to make your move that you do not fumble your assignment that will divert your "Accomplishment." Always remember that your steps are methodical and beware of those who are positioned to ruin your celebration.

2. Motivational Markers

When you have successfully made your move, it is essential that you pay close attention to the Motivational Markers along the way. These markers serve in multifaceted ways to compliment and cause completion of your goals. The "Motivational Markers" are set to remind you that you have accomplished some great things prior and there is more to be ascertained. When you take a drive on the interstate, you will discover every mile there is a mile maker. They are purposely placed to remind and reveal both at the same time.

> **What Motivational Markers Remind Us Of**

The markers remind us of just how far we have traveled. On most highways, the mile markers also coordinate with the exit numbers. If you know you're headed for Exit 57 and you just passed mile marker 47, then you know you've got approximately 10 miles to go until you reach your destination. In this way, mile markers can help you keep track of where you are and how far away you are from certain exits. In life, just as on the highway, create "Motivational Markers" that assist you in knowing exactly where you are presently located. This is majorly important because it allows you to celebrate the distance you have covered. It will amaze some people how far they have travelled in pursuit of "Accomplishment." Whenever you take a moment to express gratitude for the journey you are on, new energy emerges. The horizons you have covered bring a sense of "Accomplishment" that is unparalleled. They are intentionally placed to remind you of what you need to arrive at the conclusions in life that made the most significance. Lastly, they are not placed closely by each other. Every mile you will see them. Not every ½ mile, but every mile. The consistency that this breeds is a discipline that will work in your favor for a lifetime. Resist the temptation to move the markers to temporarily aide you. Don't cheat yourself.

The "Motivational Markers" are strategically placed to remind us that we have not completed the task, but we have made some progress. These markers can be anything personally utilized to motivate yourself. Do not limit it to just anniversaries, birthdays, or special momentous occasions. It could be a daily goal, a kiss from a special person, a hug and affection while on the journey to a better place. Perhaps, for you, it was a person who listened during a climatic and crisis filled moment. The one who held your hand and it served as a calming agent to ease your fears. A small note or a handwritten letter you kept over the years. Remind yourself of that one thing that's the turning point for you- It is personally yours. Take inventory of the "Motivational Markers" in your life, because they speak volumes about you.

> ## What Motivational Markers Reveal to Us?

The great thing about these markers is that they serve a dual purpose for each us. The duality does not compete with the other, on the contrary, they actually compliment one another. While the "Motivational Markers" cause you to look back, they also reveal somethings to look forward to. They reveal how much farther you must travel to arrive at the destination desired. The revelation of the markers presents a totally new set of lens and vantage points for you. It reveals that you get an "E" for Effort and an "A" for Accomplishment. The "E" for Effort brings attention that while celebrating what this marker caused me to remember is good, but greatness is harnessed when I am focused on what is being exposed to me presently.

The goal set before me is not only to receive an "E" for Effort, but really an "A" for Accomplishment. That is the purpose of this primer, "Groomed for Greatness." The markers are presently placed to reveal the time and energy needed to arrive at Accomplishment.

Last chapter I mentioned **"Glance at the Gauges",** this principle applies here as well. When you glance at the gauges, the information provided is obligatory for success. It can be trusted and adhered to. It's data is not contrived, but rather conclusive. Not only can you trust the data, it was be tried and shown true. You have relied on these gauges in the past, and inevitably will do so in the future. The level of your motivation will determine if you can arrive at Accomplishment or if more is required. This is not a bad sign at all. In actuality, it is pertinent. If the motivation you're presently using is lower than what is needed to arrive, you will most assuredly run out. There is a unique feeling when all the fuel/motivation has been exasperated and you have not arrived at the destination desired. The revelation from these "Motivational Markers" list calculated concerns that will enable the proper decisions to be made. One of the features they reveal is the spirit of expectancy. There is an excitement that accompanies expectancy.

Motivational Markers will reveal there is more in store, and to enjoy them proceeding forward. They remove the yearning in just revisiting your past Accomplishments, but a hunger for new ones. They will properly place your obstacles and prevent them from delaying your arrival. It will even given priority to people. Some things and people must have priority if you are going to meet the goals of Accomplishment. Everyone cannot cross into Accomplishment with you. Many make the mistake of trying to take people where they were never intended to go. When this happens, frustration flirts with our fuel until we run completely out. The value in this revelation will save you countless hours of concern for those going in the opposite direction you're traveling. Believe the markers, they were strategically placed there for a purpose. New seasons and horizons should never change our destination, although departing from certain people is inevitable.

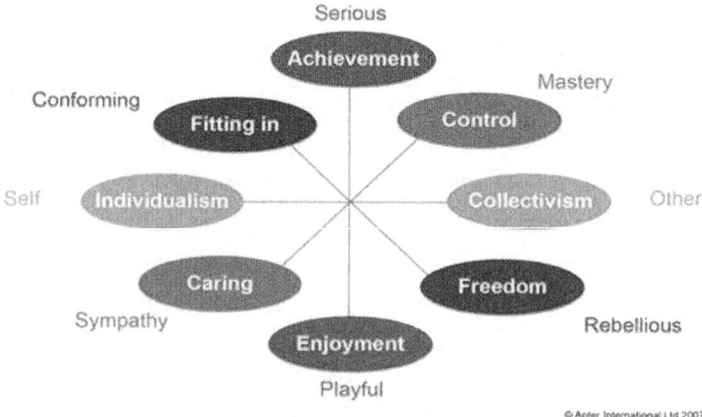

Meaningful Management

This last section on Motivational is so timely in this presentation. While being **"Groomed for Greatness"** in pursuit of Accomplishment, meaningful management is a necessity. Here is a short list:

> **Listen**

"As a leader... I have always endeavored to **listen** to what each and every person in a discussion had to say before venturing my own opinion. Oftentimes, my own opinion will simply represent a consensus of what I heard in the discussion. I always remember the axiom: a leader is like a shepherd. He stays behind the flock, letting the most nimble go out ahead, whereupon the others follow, not realizing that all along they are being directed from behind."

Nelson Mandela

In a Forbes article- "6 Ways Effective Listening Can Make You a Better Leader" stated: Listening is a leadership responsibility that does not appear in the job description. Those who do listen to their employees are in a much better position to lead the increasingly diverse and multigenerational workforce. The "one-approach-fits-all" way of thinking has become outdated and those who embrace the high art of listening are destined to be the better, more compassionate leaders.

- **Show That You Care-** "Do not view people as tools and resources for your own success- but as people and valuable assets who bring unique capabilities and aptitudes not necessarily limited to their daily functions."

- **Engage Yourself-** When you engage yourself more actively, hold yourself accountable and follow up with others; they will know that you are listening and paying attention and attempting to understand what matters most to them.

- **Be Empathetic-** Express your concerns and show others that you feel their frustrations. Empathy is a powerful display of listening.

- **Don't Judge Others-** Leaders that judge others are not listening. When leaders judge, they expose their immaturity and inability to embrace differences. Leaders must not grow complacent. The 21st century leader must embrace new ideas and ideals. They must be more active listeners, constantly learning and adapting to change.

- **Be Expansively Minded-** Great leaders are extremely mindful of their surroundings. They know how to actively listen beyond the obvious via both verbal and non-verbal communication. They acknowledge others via body language, facial expressions and nods. Leaders that are mindful are not just hearing conversations; they are listening to them and engaging in the dialogue.

- **Don't Interrupt-** Compassionate leaders listen and don't interrupt the flow of the dialogue. They embrace two-way communication and are aware that with every interruption comes disengagement. They earn respect from their peers by being a patient listener. Stay focused on what your employees are saying. Stay in the moment and be respectful of others. Listen and become a more compassionate leader.

When you implement these "Meaningful Management" tools, the gauges of your motivation will soar. It will lend permission, that while you are being **"Groomed for Greatness"**, you can groom others as well. "A boss creates fear, a leader confidence. A boss fixes blame, a leader corrects mistakes. A boss knows all, a leader asks questions. A boss makes work drudgery, a leader makes it interesting."- Russell Ewing

Stay Serious

1. Creating Momentum that last.
2. Chasing Momentum (Running after it)
3. Completing Momentum (Breaking the Finishing line tape)

Momentum is defined as –"a property of a moving body that the body has by virtue of its mass and motion and that is equal to the product of the body's mass and velocity; it determines the length of time required to bring it to rest when under the action of a constant force or moment. It is simply strength or force gained by motion or by a series of events.

One of the final, yet pivotal pieces of this puzzle, is the seriousness of creating and maintaining momentum. Many of you reading this are great at staring a project, event, or a job, but it is the ability to finish and complete the task that has become cumbersome. In these final pages, "Groomed for Greatness" will encourage you to create the proper momentum to finish.

The action steps I am about to share with you are absolutely crucial to creating a solid mindset for momentum that will produce lasting success. Vision ignites the passion within you. Nothing else will, or should for that matter, excite and create momentum in you as does the apprehension of vision, purpose, or your life's plan.

How I can define what my vision, purpose, or life's plan entails is better understood when the following questions are answered:

1. What I was created to accomplish?
2. How to accomplish what I was created for?
3. Involvement- What are the appetites of inclusion?
4. Why I am promoting the vision everywhere and in every way?

Brendan Baker of Lifehack.org, submitted an article entitled:

<u>3 Must-Do Strategies for Building Momentum in Life-</u> In the article he provides some valuable insight on the subject of momentum. Each will outline the ingredients required to produce a prolonged momentum that will reveal results. They are each detailed to eliminate the excuses that surface when success is being contemplated. Lastly, each are simplistic in presentation to resist jettison syndrome (sabotaging one's own success at the expense of self-sacrificing ideas, visions, and purpose).

1. Just do it

Nike has one of the best slogans ever: "Just do it". This is THE best method for building momentum in life. I referenced this is previous chapter on **Achievement.** Whatever it is that you want to do, whether it is starting that project that you have been putting off, perhaps it's going to the gym to help you lose that 10 pounds, perhaps it's writing the first paragraph of your next novel. Whatever it is, the best way to build momentum is to simply take action and just do it!

By taking action, you start to focus your time and energy on the things that matter most. It may feel uneasy at first, but the more time and energy given to doing it, the more comfortable you will start to become with it. Over time, the momentum builds and it feeds upon itself. It is the rush of adrenaline, a substance that is released in the body of a person who is feeling a strong emotion. The more you can 'just do it', the more and more momentum you will build, the more comfortable you will be with doing that activity or task and the more productive and effective you will be – always closer to reaching your end goal.

2. Schedule it

Perhaps you can't do it right now. In fact, of course you can't do it right now... you're reading this! But what you can do is schedule some time to do that thing that you have been putting off. Even better, make it a routine.

If you have been putting off going to the gym, schedule it in now. And stick to it. If you have trouble sticking to your schedule and not having the discipline to take action, think of your longer-term goals. Why exactly do you want to go to the gym? How would your life look and feel when you lose the 10 pounds that you want to lose? If this is not enough, don't be afraid to reward yourself. Reward yourself after each action that you take.

To build momentum, it's also no good just making an activity a 'once-off'.

DO IT EVERYDAY.

Yes, seriously, do it every day. One of the best ways for building momentum is to schedule 30 minutes every day where you will be dedicated to what it is that you want to achieve. Before you know it, after one week you would have been productive for 3.5 hours! It all adds up. Making it a routine will help embed it as a habit and help it become part of your life.

3. Learn about it

So, maybe you don't want to do exactly what it is that you should be doing. No worries. What you can do to start building momentum is to learn about what it is that you should be doing. For example, if you are struggling to get to the gym, pick up a health and fitness magazine and read up on the different exercises that you can undertake at the gym. Learn about the different programs that you can complete or the different classes that you can take part in.

Perhaps you're struggling to write the first paragraph of your next novel. Take some time out to learn about the topic that you want to be writing about. Pick up the phone and talk to someone about it. Browse a website that describes how to write a novel. Whatever it is, you can learn something about the task which will help you build momentum. Learning about the activity that you want to pursue creates neural pathways in your brain that helps you build the confidence and knowledge to be able to do what it is that you want to do.

Momentum IS beautiful. Seriously, momentum is a beautiful thing. Momentum enables you the ability to start thinking clearly, see that your goals are reachable and it gives you a sense of purpose, power and direction.

If you desire to achieve more in life, more successful, productive, effective and efficient, then I offer these 3 key strategies for building momentum for consideration.

- ❖ **Momentum helps you get over the initial 'hurdle' of not being able to start something.**
- ❖ **Momentum helps build positive thinking and energy to help you progress towards your goals.**
- ❖ **Momentum gives you belief that you can achieve what it is that you want to achieve.**

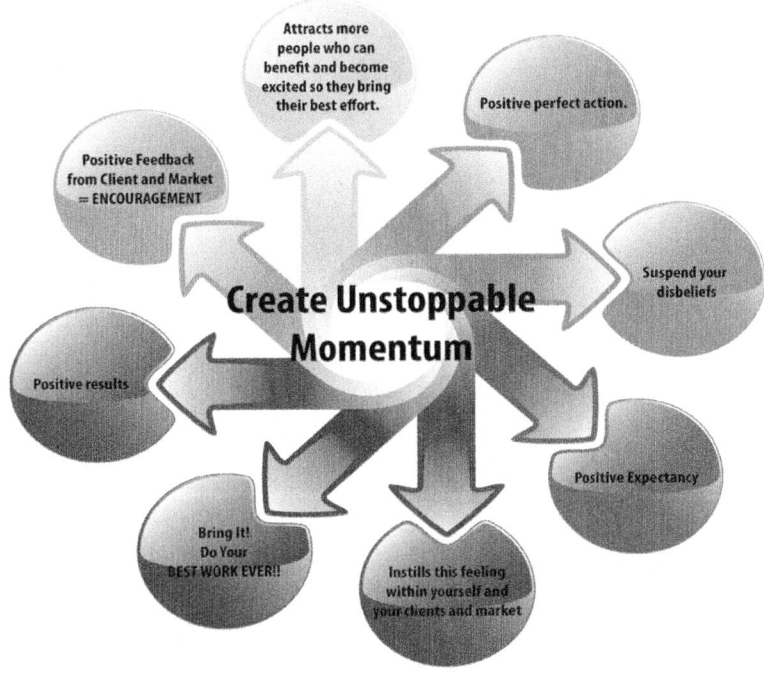

By building momentum, you are creating a world in which you are **more** productive, **more** effective and **more** efficient!

Take Actions
"Who Is Next"

Actions Steps after being- "Groomed for Greatness"

1. The Values of Greatness

2. The Vision of Greatness

3. Greatness and Vision Relationship

4. Break the Chains

The Values of Greatness

1. Greatness is the product of one's purpose.
2. Greatness is the source of true relationship
3. Greatness is calculated to one's purpose.
4. Greatness is detailed and distinguished to one's purpose.
5. Greatness never negotiates to remain status quo.
6. Greatness will always demand that you are open to change.
7. Greatness is not success, but the journey.
8. Greatness empowers people to action. What areas need immediate attention? What areas need modification?

The Vision of Greatness

1. Greatness must be seized.
2. Greatness must be streamlined.
3. Greatness must be stated.
4. Greatness must be assessed.
5. Greatness must be appraised.
6. Greatness must be appreciated.
7. Greatness must be priority.
8. Greatness must have primacy.

"Greatness and Vision"
A Relationship Cycle that Produce Results

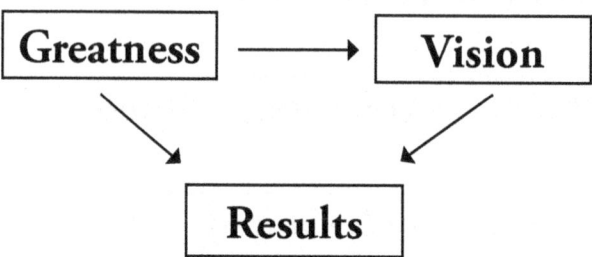

Greatness with Vision equates Results. This cycle is comprehensive and masters qualitative and quantitative abilities, to maintain sustainable results. The principles obtain here will formulate a foundation that "Greatness" can couple with vision, and catapult you into continued success. Greatness harnessed alone will lead to frustration. Vision harnessed alone will lead to irritation. This combination will equip you with the following results:

- ❖ **Recognize It**- Greatness will only speak the vision to the visionary. Only share your passion and purpose details with others who flow comprehending greatly.

- ❖ **Relate It**- Greatness will demand that you write the vision. Secondly, prepare to articulate the vision you were instructed to write. Discernment is key here.

- ❖ **Release It**- After writing it and formulating the vision in articulation, get ready to release it. Make it understandable. Proof your purpose and passion.

- ❖ **Receive It**- Being cautious and careful at this point is critical. The decision of who you will delegate to demands that you do so. Your vision of **Greatness** cannot be contained in every container. Choose wisely.

- ❖ **Read It**- Those who are privileged to receive your vision of **Greatness** should know that they are chosen and not just selected. Their responsibility is to read what was received with excitement.

- ❖ **Run With It**- This is the response of the reader. This action validates what was received, has been read. If the person reading it and does not run with it, they were not the right recipient.

Break the Chains

Break these Chains to Achieve Greatness in Your Life

Break the Chain of Loss

"The best way to guarantee a loss is to quit"- Morgan Freeman

Break the Chain of Lethargy

"Great minds are to make others great. Their superiority is to be used, not to break the multitude to intellectual vassalage, not to establish over them a spiritual tyranny, but to rouse them from lethargy, and to aid them to judge themselves."- William Ellery Channing

Break the Chain of Loneliness

"Loneliness and the feeling of being unwanted is the most terrible poverty."- Mother Teresa

Break the Chain of Lack

"The difference between a successful person and others is not a lack of strength, not a lack of knowledge, but rather a lack of will."- Vince Lombardi

Break the Chain of Limits

The difference between stupidity and genius is that genius has its limits.- Albert Einstein

BREAK EVERY CHAIN

you got the makings of
GREATNESS
in you,
BUT YOU GOT TO TAKE
the helm and chart
YOUR OWN COURSE.
STICK TO IT,
NO MATTER the squalls!
DIZRADIO.COM

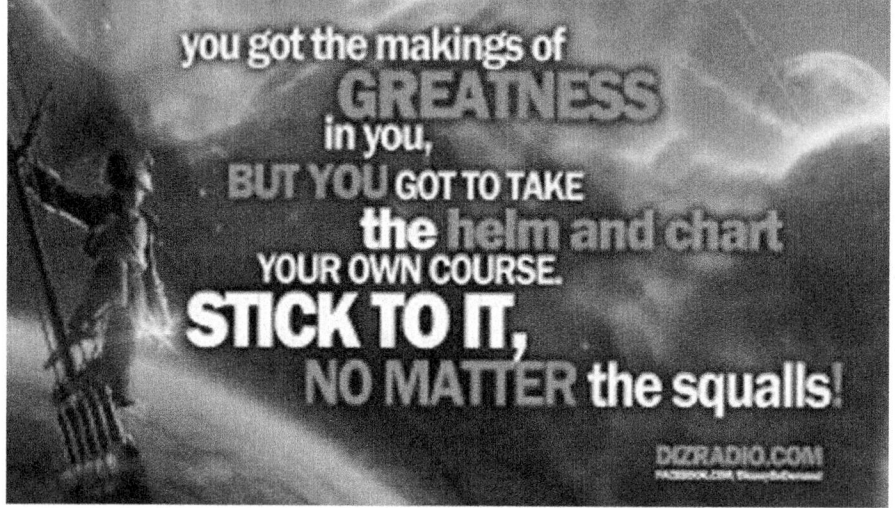

A Word from the Author

There is no upper limit to what individuals are capable of doing with their minds. There is no age limit that bars them from beginning. There is no obstacle that cannot be overcome if they persist and believe. — H.G. Wells

Thinking is key for your success or the reasoning for failure.

God will allow you to think as little of Him as you choose, or as BIG as you choose. It is the size of your thoughts of God that will control your psyche. Now the way you think of God will guide the way you think of yourself. When your perception of the Creator is limited, the scope of the creation is thus the same. Because, God will allow you to walk in the concept you accept.

You have the uniqueness of your thoughts, and I have the uniqueness of mine. When we come together (that is called fellowship "koinania") to exchange concepts to better one another. Here is the reason why, because your thoughts are not entire or total. So you can share your thoughts (praise, testimony, worship) with me and me with you, so that we might construct a view of God who is bigger than both of us!

Listen, I have an idiosyncratic construct of God. I am entitled to my construct of God. You have your own construct of God and should never allow anyone to force their construct (ideas, theory's, concepts, or thinking) upon you at the expense of committing spiritual suicide of your own thinking! Because you need my construct to complete yours and I need yours to complete mine. No one should ever compete with you over your thinking, but rather compliment you.

> "It's not the art, it's the heart. What [God] reads during our worship is the inner attitude. Worship is spiritual; it's organic; it's relational."
>
> — LaMar Boschman

This project is proof positive that you can accomplish anything that you preserve to. I am grateful for your support and it is my sincere prayer that every sentence contained within this book will speak volumes to you. It is my hope that the seeds of greatness deposited into your life via this book will enhance and enlighten the greatness in you.

Dr. Kris F. Erskine

About the Author

Dr. Kris F. Erskine, Pastor

Bethel Missionary Baptist Church- Pratt- Birmingham, AL 35173

Dr. Kris Erskine is a native of Birmingham, Alabama. He currently serves (2014) with his Pastor of thirty two (33) years, Dr. T.L. Lewis as Pastor of Operations at the Bethel Baptist Church-Pratt. He served the Bethany Baptist Church in the village of Harlem for six (6) years. His commitment to preaching and teaching spans 25 & pastoring 20 years. Dr. Erskine has matriculated & received degrees from Tuskegee University, Birmingham Baptist Bible College, and University of Alabama at Birmingham, The Birmingham Easonian Baptist Seminary- 1997, Masters of Theology from Andersonville Baptist Theological Seminary of Andersonville, GA. 2001, a Doctorate of Theology from St. Thomas Christian College in Jacksonville, FL. in May 2005, a fellowship with concentration in Pastoral Studies/Traumatic Psychosis at Union Theological Seminary & The Jewish Theological Seminary in New York- June 2011, and presently pursuing a Ph.D at Union with a concentration in Social Justice with a Global Emphasis. His commitment to academia has led to additional studies at Beeson Divinity School at Samford University in Birmingham, Alabama.

Dr. Erskine oversees the multifarious ministry at Bethel that highlights community involvement, hundreds of ministries, and small groups to service its growing discipleship. The multi-million dollar facility and the mega-size membership only compliments the holiness and heritage that is a proven hallmark.

Dr. Erskine's ministry has global impact having traveled to several continents declaring the Gospel with extensive time working in Haiti & Jamaica. He serves as Chairman/Board member & spokesman of numerous Organizations in the state and nation; NAACP, American Cancer Society, Rainbow Push Coalition, 1000 Churches Connected, Birmingham Police Community Chaplain, Bryan-College Station, TX Police Chaplain, United States Service Academy Board, Advisory Board Member Texas A&M University, Community Collaborative Board-Columbia University, Harlem Congregations for Community Improvement, St. Luke's Hospital Ministerial Board of NY, & MPAC (Mobilizing Preachers And Communities) to name a few.

Dr. Erskine is co-author of a book "The Dilemmas of Being an African American Male in the New Millennium" with Dr. Chance Lewis- Associate Professor of Teaching and Urban Education at Texas A&M University addressing the ills of the African American community with emphasis on boys and men. He recently released his second book- "Groomed for Greatness."

He is currently in the writing stages of other new solo projects "Transitions" "Single-Sons" and "The It Factor" scheduled for the fall of 2015. Dr. Erskine is also a spotlight writer for the online Gospel Magazine "The Root."

Dr. Erskine completed the Dean's Certification Program of the SSPB-NBC, USA in December 2013 in Nashville, TN, conducted a certified school in March 2014, as serves as Certified Dean of the National Baptist Convention USA, Inc. He is honored to serve on the staff and as an Instructor for the National Baptist Congress of Christian Education.

He married the lovely Loretta Gaines-Erskine on October 12, 1996. They are proud parents of two wonderful children, a son- Kristian Gabriel and a daughter- Alayna Gabrielle.

Chance W. Lewis, Ph.D. (Author)
Kris F. Erskine, Th.D. (Author)
ISBN: 0-7414-4893-9 ©2008
Price: $19.95
Book Size: 5.5" x 8.5", 111 pages
Category/Subject: SELF-HELP / Personal Growth / Success

The African American male is in a state of crisis! This powerful book explores the issues and eloquently provides real solutions to change the lives of this population. Blending academia and the anointing is exceptional. It is certain to keep you amazed at the heart the authors have for men. From dilemmas to directions: the keys to survival.

CPSIA information can be obtained
at www.ICGtesting.com
Printed in the USA
LVOW05*0918120217
524024LV00009B/111/P

9 781495 807381